# GRANDMOTHER'S RECIPES

For my mother
Marjorie
In memory of her mother
Mary Jane

*Two remarkable Wiltshire women*

It isn't so much the achievement,
It's the aim that matters more,
It's harder to sail the ocean,
Than to bring your boat to shore.
So never be weary of doing
In your hurry to be done,
There is bound to be heavy fighting
If a battle's to be won.

*Entry by Mary Jane in Marjorie's autograph album*
*Feb 4th 1934.*

# Grandmother's Recipes

∾

## The Receipt-Book
## of Mary Jane Stratton

∾

## Katy Jordan

First published in the United Kingdom in 2003 by
The Hobnob Press, PO Box 1838, East Knoyle, Salisbury SP3 6FA

British Library Cataloguing in Publication Data
A catalogue record for this book is available from the British Library.

ISBN 0-946418-17-9

Typeset in Scala and Bodoni
Typesetting and origination by John Chandler
Printed in Great Britain by Salisbury Printing Company Ltd, Salisbury

# Contents

Introduction                                    ix
The Life of Mary Jane Stratton         xi
Testing, Testing – one hundred         xxi
    years on
Weights and Measures                    xxiv

❧

## The Recipes

### 1 Main Courses & Savouries        1
Roman Pie                                     3
Devilling                                       5
Stewed Rabbit                                6
Pulled Fish                                     7
Mrs Fearon's Fish Soufflé                9
Tomato Soufflé                              10
Mrs Sladen's Cheese Soufflé          12
    Mrs Sladen                             13
Mrs Sladen's Salad Dressing          14
Indian Toast                                  16
Cheese Canapées                          17

❧

### 2 Baked Puddings                  19
Nassaw Pudding                           21
Marmalade Pudding                      22
Orange Pudding                           23
Derbyshire Pudding                      25

At a Devizes School                      26
Princess Amelia's Puddings          27
Devonshire Pudding                     28
Sultana Pudding                           29
Gooseberry & Rhubarb
    Turnovers                               31

❧

### 3 Boiled or Steamed
    Puddings                               33
Chocolate Pudding                       35
Iris Pudding                                 36
Marmalade Pudding                     37
Ashfield Pudding                         38
Blackberry Pudding                      40
Paradise Pudding                         41
Bachelor's Pudding                      43
Fig Pudding                                 44
Severn Cup Pudding                    45
Mrs Loveredge's Christmas
    Pudding                                46
    Lady Jemima Johnson           47

❧

### 4 Set Desserts                       49
Cabinet Pudding                          51
Crystal Palace Pudding                53
Caramel Pudding                         54

| | |
|---|---|
| Chocolate Cream | 56 |
| Mrs Gale's Rhubarb Sponge | 57 |
| Raspberry Sponge | 59 |
| Lemon Cream | 60 |
| Lemon or Orange Solid | 62 |
| Apple Jelly | 63 |
| Egg Jelly | 64 |
| Apricot Eggs | 66 |

∞

**5 Cakes Large and Small** — 67

| | |
|---|---|
| Jam Sandwich | 69 |
| Phyllis's Sponge Cake | 70 |
| Swiss Roll | 71 |
| Mocha Cake | 73 |
| Coffee Butter & Icing | 75 |
| Madeira Cake | 77 |
| Orange Cake | 78 |
| Manchester Cake | 80 |
| Ginger Bread Cake | 82 |
| Scarborough Cake | 83 |
| Phyllis's Lemon Cake | 84 |
| Military Tartlets | 85 |
| Phyllis's Queen Cakes | 87 |
| Chocolate Cakes | 88 |
| Chocolate Icing | 89 |
| Mrs Gale's Rice Cakes | 90 |
| Drop Cakes | 91 |
| Mrs Meyrick's German Shortbread | 92 |
| Scones | 94 |
| Lottie's Doughnuts | 95 |
| **Rose and Lottie** | 97 |
| Rose's Sultana Cake | 98 |
| Rose's Pound Cake | 99 |
| German Pound Cake | 100 |

| | |
|---|---|
| Mrs Parker's Norwich Cake | 101 |
| Fruit cake | 102 |

∞

**6 Chutneys & Preserves** — 103

| | |
|---|---|
| Apple Chutney | 105 |
| Hot Tomato Chutney | 107 |
| Sweet Tomato Chutney | 109 |
| Mrs Felce's Green Tomato Chutney | 110 |
| **Mrs Felce** | 111 |
| Eva's Beetroot Chutney | 112 |
| **Eva and her Family** | 113 |
| Lady Malcolm's Mincemeat | 115 |
| **Lady Wilhelmina Charlotte Malcolm** | 116 |
| Mrs Woolfrey's Bottled Gooseberries Rhubarb & Damsons | 117 |
| Mrs. Felce's method of preserving French Beans | 118 |
| To Preserve Vegetable Marrow | 118 |
| Mrs Smith's Pickled Marrow | 118 |

∞

**7 Jams, Jellies & Marmalades** — 119

| | |
|---|---|
| Apricot Jam | 121 |
| Blackberry Jam | 122 |
| Ginger Rhubarb | 123 |
| Apple Jelly | 125 |
| Gooseberry Jelly | 126 |
| Dundee Marmalade | 128 |
| **Beckhampton Racing Stables** | 130 |
| Lemon Cheese Cake | 131 |
| Green Tomato Jam | 132 |

**8  Boiled Sweets**                      *133*
Toffee                                     *134*

Elderberry Wine                           *138*
Orange Wine                               *138*
Parsnip Wine                              *139*
Plum Wine                                 *139*
Potato Wine                               *139*

**9  Country Wines, Beers &**
**   Spirits**                            *135*
Apple Beer                                *136*
Apple Wine                                *136*
Beetroot Wine/Mock Port                   *136*
Blackberry Wine                           *136*
Blackcurrant Wine                         *137*
Carrot Wine                               *137*
Damson Wine                               *137*
Dandelion Wine                            *138*

Raspberry Wine                            *140*
Redcurrant Wine                           *140*
Rhubarb Wine                              *141*
Sloe Wine                                 *141*
Sloe Gin                                  *141*
Whiskey Wine                              *142*

*Acknowledgements*                        *143*
*Bibliography*                            *144*
*Index*                                   *145*

Throughout this book illustrations of Edwardian kitchen utensils, advertisements and quotations are taken from Mrs Beeton's *Book of household management* and *Every-day cookery*, 1907 editions.

Ginger Bread Cake.

1 lb of Treacle
¼ lb of Butter
¼ lb. Sugar.
1½ lb of Flour
½ oz Ginger.
½ oz all Spice.
1. tea spoon full of Baking Powder.
¼ " " " " Carbonate Soda.
¼ pt of milk.
1 egg.
Put the Butter into the Flour. mix all
the other ingredients in by degrees
Bake in a Slow oven about 1 hour.
it usually takes much longer.

Solid Custard

1½ pts of milk poured boiling hot on 1 oz
Jelatine + yolks of 4 eggs add sugar +
Lemon peel to taste keep it stirred
while boiling to thicken Place in
a mould when cold turn out.

*A page from Mary Jane's receipt book*

# Introduction

**E**arly in 2002, my mother gave me a battered old black exercise book, written throughout in her mother's distinctive handwriting. I had just begun researching our family history, and she thought that I might like to keep the book along with the photos and other family memorabilia. Of course I was fascinated, for I had never known my grandmother, who had died four years before I was born. A book that she had written herself would be a very personal link to her, whatever its contents; but this was a real breath of bygone days, each page filled with recipes – or *receipts*, as she called them – collected when she was in service between 1901 and 1913. Mary Jane Stratton, always a benevolent, if remote, influence on my life, was about to take centre stage.

My grandmother left us very few tangible reminders of her life: some photographs, a book she won as a prize at school, a few pieces of jewellery including the little wooden locket that her husband Ned carried all through the First World War; a Staffordshire Red Riding Hood figure; and her old recipe book.

Looking through the book, I saw that it was full of delicious recipes for cakes, savouries, puddings, desserts, chutneys, jellies and country wines. As I continued turning the pages I found myself wanting to go into the kitchen and try them out. Then the thought crossed my mind: 'I think there's a book in this'.

And here it is. My grandmother's recipes: the receipt-book of Mary Jane Stratton.

*Katy Jordan*
*1st September 2003*

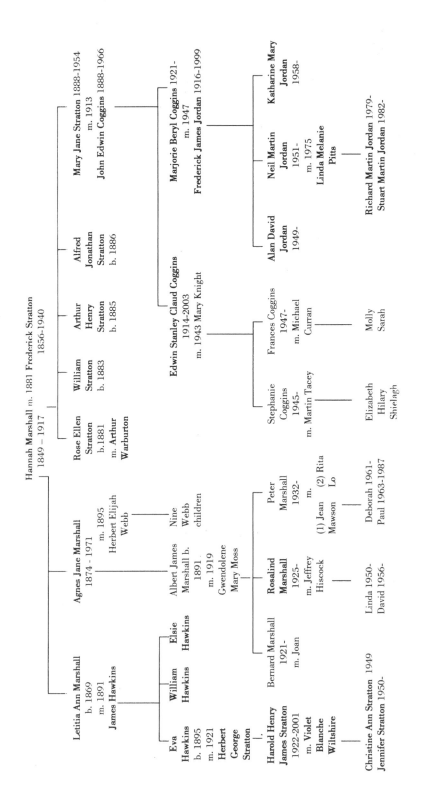

Hannah Marshall m. 1881 Frederick Stratton
1849 – 1917                                    1856-1940

**Letitia Ann Marshall**
b. 1869
m. 1891
**James Hawkins**

**Agnes Jane Marshall**
1874 - 1971
m. 1895
Herbert Elijah Webb

**Rose Ellen Stratton**
b.1881
m. **Arthur Warburton**

**William Stratton**
b. 1883

**Arthur Henry Stratton**
b. 1885

**Alfred Jonathan Stratton**
b. 1886

**Mary Jane Stratton** 1888-1954
m. 1913
**John Edwin Coggins** 1888-1966

**Eva Hawkins**
b. 1895
m. 1921
**Herbert George Stratton**

**William Hawkins**

**Elsie Hawkins**

Albert James Marshall b. 1891
m. 1919
Gwendolene Mary Moss

Nine Webb children

**Edwin Stanley Claud Coggins**
1914-2003
m. 1943 Mary Knight

**Marjorie Beryl Coggins** 1921-
m. 1947
**Frederick James Jordan** 1916-1999

**Harold Henry James Stratton**
1922-2001
m. **Violet Blanche Wiltshire**

**Bernard Marshall**
1921-
m. Joan

**Rosalind Marshall**
1925-
m. Jeffrey Hiscock

Peter Marshall
1932-
m.
(1) Jean Mawson   (2) Rita Lo

Stephanie Coggins
1945-
m. Martin Tacey

Frances Coggins
1947-
m. Michael Curran

**Alan David Jordan**
1949-

**Neil Martin Jordan**
1951-
m. 1975
**Linda Melanie Pitts**

**Katharine Mary Jordan**
1958-

**Christine Ann Stratton** 1949
**Jennifer Stratton** 1950-

Linda 1950-
David 1956-

Deborah 1961-
Paul 1963-1987

Elizabeth
Hilary
Shielagh

Molly
Sarah

**Richard Martin Jordan** 1979-
**Stuart Martin Jordan** 1982-

The descendants of Mary Jane's parents. Names in **bold** belong to people who are mentioned in the book.

# The Life of Mary Jane Stratton

⁕

**M**ary Jane was born in 1888, the youngest child of Frederick and Hannah Stratton. Frederick was an agricultural labourer from Honeystreet, a canal-side hamlet in the parish of Woodborough in Wiltshire's Vale of Pewsey. In 1881, aged 25, he had married Hannah Marshall, an unmarried mother nearly six years his senior. They settled down in Alton Barnes with Hannah's 6-year old daughter Agnes Jane Marshall, while just a few cottages away her 12-year old daughter Letitia Ann ('Annie') lived with Hannah's father Jonathan Marshall.

*Frederick Stratton*

Their daughter Rose Ellen was born in 1881, followed by three sons, William (1883), Arthur Henry (1885), and Alfred Jonathan (1886). Finally Mary Jane was born on 28th September 1888. By this time the family had outgrown the cottage at Alton Barnes, and was living at a house called St Margaret's ('Maggots') Castle, near Hurst Dairy in the Sands at Woodborough.

In July 1893, when she was almost five, Mary Jane entered the infant class at Woodborough Church of England Primary School. The school served the parishes of Woodborough, North Newnton, Manningford Bohune and Beechingstoke, and there were around 160 pupils split into

*Hannah Stratton*

*Woodborough Church of England School, c. 1900*

several different grades.  The headmaster was Ernest Edward Whitting, and he was supported by his wife, who was sewing mistress, and three assistant teachers, one of whom, Miss S.L. Smith, taught the infants.  The school log book, kept by the headmaster, paints a fascinating, although somewhat limited, picture of life in school in the 1890s.

   *Inspector's report of August 1893*: 'The school is in good order and has a good tone.  The instruction is very fair in quality.  While Reading and Writing have not been well taught, Spelling is Satisfactory. . . and Arithmetic is good.  The class subjects are fair and note singing is successful.  A needlework cupboard is wanted.' Of the Infant class he writes: 'Order is exact and the infants are making good progress under their new teacher', but 'The school room is not well warmed in cold weather' and 'the classroom being only 17ft by 18ft does not satisfy the requirements . . . of the code'.

   Life at school, then, could be cold and cramped, and not surprisingly, the log book records that every winter colds, 'flu, whooping cough and other illnesses afflicted both pupils and teachers.   Besides these understandable absences, students were also kept away by their parents whenever there was work to be done: on 29th September 1893, Mr Whitting records 'Attendance on Friday afternoon was 33 below the average, most of the absentees having been employed in the fields picking acorns up, which the rough wind has blown from the trees' and on Dec 17th 1896 he notes, 'this being Devizes Xmas market many of the children were away'.

   There were a number of holidays and treats for the pupils.  Less than two weeks after Mary Jane began school, all the schoolchildren were given a tea at the end of the school day.  In February 1895, school closed early for 'a Children's Entertainment, got up for the purpose of providing prizes for the most regular and deserving scholars'. In early September 1898, 'holiday was given . . . on account of the Military review at Beacon Hill, to which the whole district seems to be going'. On October 15th every year it was the annual Woodborough Feast, and there was a half-holiday for all the children.[1]

In 1901, the school leaving age was still 12 years, and the school record book notes that Mary Jane Stratton duly left on 24th May 1901 to become a Monitor. This was her first tentative step towards becoming a teacher. Monitors were untrained children who helped schoolteachers in the classroom. Later, they might sign formal indentures to become pupil-teachers and then go on to college to train as teachers. This 'was almost the only avenue to higher education open to intelligent children of the upper artisan class'.[2] But Mary Jane was a labourer's daughter, and the road to higher education proved to be beyond her reach. Her daughter Marjorie recalls that 'she should have been a teacher', and there is no doubt that she was intelligent enough; but her parents simply could not afford to support her any more, and so, like many working-class country girls, she had to go into service.

We do not know a great deal about her working life. She wrote nothing down relating to that time apart from the recipes and the names of the people who gave them to her. Mary Jane's daughter Marjorie, of course, recalls various tales that her mother told her, and from these we were able to identify five households where she had worked. The location of another workplace was found on the back of a postcard, addressed to Miss M. Stratton, and kept unnoticed for decades among the family photographs.

We know that Mary Jane worked at:-

- A school in Devizes, Wiltshire. See p. 26
- The racing stables at Beckhampton, Wiltshire. See p.130
- Lady Johnson's residence in Upton-on-Severn, Worcestershire. See pp.47-8
- Lady Malcolm's residence in Clevedon, Somerset. See p.116
- Mr. & Mrs. Gilbert Felce's residence in London. See p.111
- Rev. & Mrs. Sladen's residence in Alton Barnes, Wiltshire. See p.13

*Alton Barnes Rectory*

It may well be that Mary Jane worked in other places besides these. There are about a dozen names in her book that we cannot identify, and these are probably people with whom she worked or had dealings during her working life. Those we do know are her employers Lady Malcolm, Mrs. Felce and Mrs. Sladen, who all contributed recipes; as did her sister Rose Stratton, her cousin Charlotte Giddings, and her niece Eva Hawkins.

Mary Jane began her working life as a kitchen-maid, being trained by the cooks with whom she worked, collecting recipes and learning by observation how to manage a kitchen for a demanding employer.

> Duties of the Kitchen-Maid. – Whilst the cook is engaged with her morning duties, the kitchen- or scullery-maid is also occupied with hers. Her first duty, after the fire is lighted, is to sweep and clean the kitchen and the various offices belonging to it. This she does every morning, besides cleaning the stone steps at the entrance of the house, the halls, the passages, and the stairs, if any, which lead to the kitchen. Her general duties, besides these, are to wash and scour all these places twice a week, with the table, shelves, and cupboards. She has also to attend to the nursery and servants' hall dinners while cooking, to prepare all fish, poultry and vegetables, trim meat joints and cutlets, and do all such duties as may be assigned to her by the cook.[3]

When she was eighteen Mary Jane went for her first job as a cook, putting up her hair to make herself look older. When she got the job, she went straight out and bought a copy of *Mrs. Beeton's Book of Household Management*, and this was her guide from then on. Whenever her employer asked for anything that she had not heard of, she looked it up in Mrs. Beeton.

> Daily duties. – In those households where cook and housemaid only are kept, the general custom is that the cook shall look after the dining room. . . after having lighted her kitchen fire, brushed the range, and cleaned the hearth, [she will] proceed to prepare for breakfast. She will thoroughly rinse the kettle, and set it to boil. She may then perhaps have to go to the breakfast-room, and there make things ready for the breakfast. Attention must also be given to sweeping the hall, shaking the hall mats, which she must afterwards put back in their places.
>
> The cook usually answers the bells and single knocks at the door in the early part of the morning, as the tradesmen, which whom it is her more special business to speak, call at these hours.
>
> The preparation of dinner is the most important part of the cook's work, wherein she begins to feel the responsibility of her situation, as she has to see to the dressing and serving of those dishes, which her skill and ingenuity have prepared.[4]

What might Mary Jane expect to earn as a kitchen maid or cook at that time? Servants usually lived in their employer's house, with free board and lodging, known as 'everything found'. They would probably have to pay for their own working uniform, however. Mrs. Beeton gives us guidance as to the proper wages to be paid to different types of servant. These are the rates from London and the surrounding area: outside London the wages would be lower. We should not be too surprised to see that male servants earned more than females in equivalent roles:

- House Steward (male)     £60 - £100 p.a.
- Housekeeper (female)     £30 - £60 p.a.
- Valet (male)             £35 - £50 p.a.
- Lady's maid              £25 - £40 p.a.
- Cook (male)              £100 and above p.a.
- Cook (female)            £20 – £60 p.a.
- Kitchen maid             £16 - £28 p.a. [5]

It was when she was working as cook for Mrs Sladen in Alton Barnes that Mary Jane met a smart young man of military bearing who called every day at the Rectory to deliver the post. This was John Edwin (Ned) Coggins, an ex-soldier of the Royal Berkshire Regiment, who came from a family of postal workers in Mortimer, Berkshire.

Ned began working as rural postman based at Oare in February 1912, earning 19 shillings a week, plus 1 shilling a week allowance for washing his bicycle. He cycled every day from Oare Post Office out to the Altons, delivering the post to a number of villages along the way.[6] He was soon smitten by the pretty young cook at Alton Rectory, and their engagement photograph (page xx) shows a handsome, well-matched young couple.

John Edwin Coggins and Mary Jane Stratton were married on the 14th June 1913 at the altar of Woodborough church. Ned's brother Claude was best man, and Mary Jane's niece Eva Hawkins was bridesmaid. They began their married life in Oare, living conveniently next door to the Post Office.

When war broke out in 1914, Mary Jane was pregnant with their first child. Ned was in the reserves, and was called up immediately, so Mary Jane had to manage on her own. She went home to her parents to have the baby, as many women did with their first child, and Edwin Stanley Claud Coggins was born in Honeystreet on 9th November 1914. It was not an easy birth, and we can see how tired Mary Jane looks in the

*Woodborough Church around the time of Mary Jane's wedding*

photograph she had taken soon after. She took the baby home to Oare, but her father Frederick walked every day from Honeystreet to Oare to see her and make sure that she and little Stanley were well.

*Mary Jane with Stanley*

Ned came home on leave the following year, when Stanley was nearly a year old, and the family were united for the first time. Sergeant Coggins already looks haunted by his experiences in the trenches. He returned to the front, and served thoughout the war, avoiding major injury. When the war was over, he served with the army of occupation in Germany, and it was not until 1919 that he came home to his family and job in Oare. He and Mary Jane were not parted again while she lived.

*Ned, Mary Jane and Stanley in 1915*

Young Stanley was not used to having his father about the house, and it took him a while to adjust to him. Ned was stricter than Stanley's mother and grandparents were. Soon Mary Jane began to find that a photograph of Ned was often turned to face the wall. All became clear one day when she found young Stanley turning the picture around, saying, "I don't like you, our old dad, coming home and bossing I about!"[7]

Ned and Mary Jane's second child Marjorie Beryl Coggins was born on 7th November 1921, and so their family was complete. They lived for a while in a council

house in Alton Priors, but they were able to
return home to Oare when Sir Geoffrey Fry
offered them the rental of one of a new
pair of cottages he was building on the
Oare House estate in Rudge Lane. The
architect was Clough Williams-Ellis, the
designer of Portmeirion, who had done
other work in the village. The head
gardener and his wife were to have one
cottage, and the postman and his family
the other.

So Mary Jane, Ned and family
moved to Orchard Cottage, which
remained the family home until 1975.
They were not well off, but the garden was
big and they could grow fruit and
vegetables there, and on their allotment
in the village. Ned also supplemented
his Post Office earnings by mending

*Ned in 1919 at the end of the war*

shoes, a trade he had learned in the army. Mary Jane was a good manager, and kept
her accounts scrupulously. Her thrift and good management skills were to become
vital in the years ahead.

*Postman Coggins outside Oare post office, c. 1922. He wears the old-style uniform with
shako and puttees.*

Mary Jane could see that education was the only way for her children to get on in the world, and she was determined that they should have the best she could afford to give them. Both Stanley and Marjorie attended Marlborough Grammar School, which cost 2 guineas a term each; and they also both had music lessons, which cost another 2 guineas a term each. People in the village laughed at Mary Jane because she had not sent her children out to work as soon as she could.

*Ned and Mary Jane with Stanley and Marjorie*

They must have laughed even more when she scrimped and saved for three years so that she could send her son Stanley to do a general degree in education at the University of Bristol. This was a time of great hardship for the family, as half of Ned's earnings went to pay for Stanley's lodgings in Bristol. They had three lodgers, and Mary Jane went picking currants each summer to earn money. She didn't have a new dress for three years, and when she did get one it cost just 5 shillings (25p) from Marks & Spencer's. Once, at her wits' end, Mary Jane said that she didn't know how

*Marjorie's wedding to Frederick Jordan at Pewsey in 1947. Mary Jane, by now very unwell, stands beside Ned (third and second from right).*

she was going to manage, but Ned replied, 'Well, you sent him there. You'll have to manage.' He was not criticising her, just making a statement of fact; and with Ned's support, she did indeed manage, and Stanley was qualified as a teacher.

The laughter in the village stopped for good a few years later, when news got round that Stanley Coggins had become headmaster of a large school in Leicester. Mary Jane's belief in education was vindicated.

Her daughter Marjorie, like her mother, wanted to become a teacher, but Mary Jane was older now, and could not face the hardship of finding the money to pay for her to go to college. So Marjorie went into the Civil Service in Reading, and lodged with relatives of Ned's. But she came home again in 1941 to help her father care for her mother, for Mary Jane had developed both rheumatoid and osteo-arthritis. Marjorie was offered a job in Stanton St. Bernard as an uncertificated teacher, and this proved to be the start of her long career in teaching. There are many people from the Vale of Pewsey who can remember being taught by Mrs. Jordan.

By 1950, both Stanley and Marjorie had married and had children. Stanley and his family lived near his school in Leicester, but Marjorie and her husband Fred and their family were living with Ned and Mary Jane at Orchard Cottage. Marjorie kept house for her parents, brought up her two sons, and nursed her mother, who now had developed leukaemia.

Mary Jane died after a long illness on 30th August 1954, aged 65 years. Her ashes are buried in her father Frederick's grave, in Woodborough churchyard, close to the church where she and Ned were married.

These, then, are some of the events in the life of Mary Jane Stratton. But what was she like as a person?

Marjorie recalls that while she was well, her mother was very involved in village life, and sang in the church choir. She was always ready to help out with refreshments at village socials. Marjorie's husband Fred used to tell a story about Mary Jane that shows that she could also be crushingly honest. He had just finished redecorating her room with wallpaper and a pretty border. There was not quite enough of the border to go all the way round, so he tucked the 6-inch gap away where it would be least noticeable, intending to buy some more to finish the job. Mary Jane came in to inspect the room, turned round, pointed straight at the gap, and said, "You missed that bit." It was a moment he never forgot!

The love and respect both Mary Jane's children showed and still show for her, are the best evidence that she was a wise and loving woman. And she was not by nature solemn. Mary Jane's niece Rosalind Hiscock, who stayed at Orchard Cottage many times in her teens, recalls: "Aunt Jennie was great fun, always laughing. She didn't make a big fuss about her illness, just laughed it off. She always wanted to know everything that was going on in the village. When Marjorie and I went to dances, she used to wait up for us, and we couldn't go to bed until she had heard all about it."[8]

Most of all, the choices Mary Jane made in her life show that she was a person of vision and determination who, at no small cost to herself, enabled her children to make the most of their educational opportunities. Stanley and Marjorie inherited her respect for education, and through them Mary Jane has touched the lives of all her grandchildren and great-grandchildren. It is, I think, just the inheritance she would have wished for her family.

[1] WSRO F8/500/297/1/1: Woodborough CE school log book, 1873-1917.
[2] Horn, Pamela (1989). *The Victorian and Edwardian schoolchild.* Gloucester: Alan Sutton, p.177.
[3] Beeton, Mrs (1907), *Mrs Beeton's book of household management.* London: Ward, Lock, p.38.
[4] Beeton, Mrs (1907), *Mrs Beeton's book of household management.* London: Ward, Lock, p.38.
[5] Beeton, Mrs (1907), *Mrs Beeton's book of household management.* London: Ward, Lock, p.16.
[6] WSRO 3144/2/2: Post Office, appointments of rural postmen.
[7] Stanley Coggins (2002), *pers. comm.*                    [8] Rosalind Hiscock (2003), *pers. comm.*

*Ned and Mary Jane around
the time of their engagement,
1913*

# Testing, Testing – one hundred years on

So how exactly does one go about getting a hundred-year-old, hand-written cookery book ready for publication? First, you need a publisher. I approached John Chandler of the Hobnob Press at an opportune moment, for it turned out that he had been thinking about publishing a cookery book. He was interested in the idea of a recipe book with a strong element of Wiltshire family history, and after some discussion about how the book might be structured, we agreed to go ahead. Next, you need recipes that really work. It was obvious from the beginning that I couldn't simply transcribe the recipes and leave them as they were, as they were designed for cooks working in very different kitchens from our own.

The most obvious difference was the cooker: Mary Jane would have been using a solid fuel range, or just possibly, in London, a gas cooker. Electric cookers were available in the 1900s, but were very unusual and electricity itself was very expensive. Not only was the cooker very different, but my grand-mother's cooking instructions were not always helpful: "Bake for 1 hour in a moderate oven. It usually takes much longer," she wrote in one recipe, and in another just "Bake as usual". These vague directions would be no help at all for modern cooks, already uncertain about what temperature the oven should be. I would need to add cooking times and temperatures to every recipe.

Also I had a shrewd suspicion that many of the ingredients Mary Jane used would be subtly different from our own. She bought gelatine in sheets; we buy it as powder in sachets. Do they behave in the same way? Chocolate Menier in her time was sold in sticks; we find it wrapped in bars. Does a bar of chocolate contain as much as a stick? What about dried apricots? Were they very much drier than those we have today? Were they as sugary? Would our organic apricots be similar? As I turned the pages of the receipt-book, such questions came thick and fast.

It was clear that I would have to select the recipes carefully, and then get them all tested, so as to ensure that they would work for 21st-century cooks using 21st-century ingredients in 21st-century kitchens. I transcribed the entire book, grouping the recipes by type – puddings, cakes, preserves and so on – to see exactly what I had. Then I selected just over 100 recipes for testing, choosing a good variety of dishes, favouring ones with complete lists of ingredients and at least adequate cooking instructions.

Next I set about pulling together a team of people to help test the recipes, targeting family, friends, and colleagues. Once they heard about the book, people were very keen to help, and I soon had a team of good everyday cooks lined up ready to go. October 2002 saw me emailing recipe-testing forms to people all over the country, from Sherborne to Edinburgh. Some took just one recipe, others took several, and one enthusiast took twelve! Along with the recipe sheets I gave them some guidelines:

> *You have two jobs: to test the recipes, and to 'translate' the ingredients and method when necessary into something easy for a modern cook to follow. . . Please make full use of our modern cooking methods and appliances when they are appropriate and helpful e.g. use a pressure cooker to boil a suet pudding. Mary Jane cooked on a solid fuel range, but we don't have to!*

Gradually, as the months passed, the recipes began to filter back to me, some by post, some by email, some hand-written and passed to me direct. It was fascinating to see how differently people worked. Some testers were purists, sticking strictly to the recipes and ingredients; others suggested variations or different flavourings. I had included a section on the recipe-testing form for their comments: some were very brief, or non-existent; other testers wrote enthusiastically and at length. I have edited their recipes and comments as little as possible, and so you will hear their different voices as you read through the book.

Meanwhile I was testing recipes too, and at the same time reading about the social conditions during the Edwardian period. I wanted background information about Mary Jane's life and work. What was it like to work as a cook in Edwardian times? How much would she have earned? What equipment did she have? Quite a few of the recipes had names alongside them: Phyllis, Mrs Fearon, Mrs Felce, Mrs Loveredge, Rose, Eva and Lady Malcolm, among others. I wanted to find out who these people were, if possible: were they friends, relatives, colleagues or employers? Where did Mary Jane work? Did she stay in Wiltshire, or go further afield? Who were her employers?

As the weeks passed I found myself delving into libraries and archives in Trowbridge and Taunton; emailing for information to Worcestershire Record Office and the Upton-on-Severn website; briefing a friend in Edinburgh to do some research for me in the National Library of Scotland; and going with another friend to read the inscriptions on every gravestone in a Clevedon churchyard. I was also spending hours on the 1901 census service, ordering marriage certificates from the

GRO, trawling through parish registers, and interviewing family members for memories of Mary Jane.

I also initiated a nationwide search for a 1907 edition of Mrs Beeton's *Book of Household Management*, the book that Mary Jane used as her guide through her career as a cook. It was very elusive, but I finally located a copy just down the road at the library of Bath Spa University College. It proved to be crucial in setting my grandmother's working life in context, as it contains masses of advice to employers and employees, practical advice for kitchen-maids and cooks, and guidance about the kinds of dishes they had to prepare. I have used quotations from Mrs. Beeton to start each of the sections of recipes, and other brief quotations throughout the book give a sense of what it was like to work in an Edwardian kitchen.

Now all these different threads have come together. Over 100 recipes have been interwoven with family and social history, and the result is, I hope, a recipe book with added value: plenty of recipes that you can try with confidence; plus a flavour of what life was like for an ordinary Wiltshire woman in service in the early 20th century.

# Weights and Measures

Mary Jane, of course, worked in pounds and ounces. She also measured quantities in pints, quarts, gills, teacups, wine-glasses, table-, dessert-, tea- and salt-spoons, and occasionally specifies 'a little piece of butter about the size of a walnut'.

    To add to the confusion, while most of my testers happily worked in pounds and ounces, a few (younger) ones used kilogrammes and grammes. I have chosen to give imperial weights and measures, as they are an integral part of the original recipes. So ingredients are measured in pounds and ounces, pints and fluid ounces. If you prefer metric measures, there are approximate conversion tables below.

    I have given all oven temperatures in °C, °F, and Gas marks. When the tester was cooking on an Aga, I have also included the Aga cooking instructions.

| Weights | | Volume | |
|---|---|---|---|
| ½ oz | 10 g | 2 fl oz | 55 ml |
| 1 | 25 | 3 | 75 |
| 1 ½ | 40 | 5 (¼ pint) | 150 |
| 2 | 50 | 10 (½ pint) | 275 |
| 2 ½ | 60 | 15 (¾ pint) | 425 |
| 3 | 75 | 20 (1 pint) | 570 |
| 4 | 110 | | |
| 4 ½ | 125 | Measurements | |
| 5 | 150 | 1 inch | 2.5 cm |
| 6 | 175 | 2 | 5 |
| 7 | 200 | 3 | 7.5 |
| 8 | 225 | 4 | 10 |
| 9 | 250 | 5 | 13 |
| 10 | 275 | 6 | 15 |
| 12 | 350 | 7 | 18 |
| 1 lb | 450 | 8 | 20 |

# THE RECIPES

In the sections that follow you will find each recipe treated in the same way.

1. Mary Jane's original receipt, with her own spelling, capitalisation and turn of phrase.
2. The tester's ingredients and method.
3. Any comments on the recipe that the tester wanted to share with you.
4. The type of cooker used to test the recipe.
5. The tester's name.

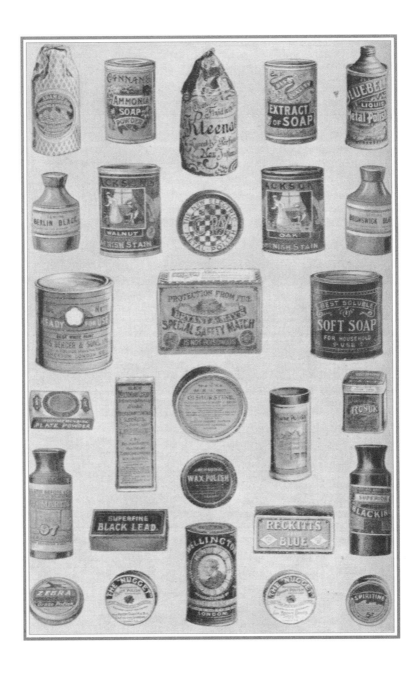

# 1
# Main Courses & Savouries

❧

There is no bird, nor any bird's egg, that is known to be poisonous, though they may, and often do, become unwholesome by reason of the food that the birds eat. . . It is considered by some fowl-keepers that the flesh of a healthy well-fed fowl, which has lived a free, out-of-door life, is both in flavour and wholesomeness preferable to a bird kept in confinement and compulsorily fed.

The wild rabbit is a native of Great Britain, and is found in large numbers. . . The flesh of the wild rabbit is darker than that of the domesticated species, and is by some considered to possess a higher flavour, although neither so white nor so delicate.

As an article of nourishment, fish is less satisfying and less stimulating than butcher's meat. . . It is, however, a matter of common experience that in fishing-towns, where little or no other animal food is taken, the health and vigour of the inhabitants are excellent. . . The first necessity for fish is that it should be fresh. Stiffness and rigidity of the flesh are a sure guide, for *RIGOR MORTIS* passes off in the course of time, and the flesh then becomes flabby.

The success of soufflés and soufflé-omelets depends largely upon the whites of the eggs being whisked to a proper degree of stiffness. When the eggs are fresh, all that is necessary to ensure this is careful separation from the yolks, the addition of a pinch of salt, and that the air whipped in is as cold as possible. . . Soufflés should be served as soon as they are done, for if over-cooked or allowed to stand, they lose some of their lightness.

In Italy, and especially with Neapolitans, macaroni is a popular article of food. It is prepared from hard varieties of wheat, which is ground to a fine meal and made into a stiff paste with a small quantity of water. Macaroni is a nutritious and wholesome food, and is used for thickening soups, for puddings, and other forms of cookery.

*Mrs. Beeton (1907), various pages*

Mrs. Beeton gives us sound advice on some of the major ingredients to be found in the savoury dishes that make up this section.

Mary Jane was quite selective about the meat dishes she collected in her receipt-book, choosing meats that she might easily be able to find for her own future household. Country people kept chickens, and rabbits were abundant in the fields, along with other more exclusive game. When Ned Coggins went on his postal round with their little dog Roy for company, Roy would often bring him a rabbit or pheasant. This would be stowed for safety in the Victorian postbox at West Stowell, and collected on their way home. In February 1948, the family at Orchard Cottage ate 'Postbox' pheasant for dinner, and then Marjorie went to Savernake hospital to have Alan, Ned and Mary Jane's first grandson.

# Roman Pie

Boil Maccronie make white sauce take Chicken Maccronie grated cheese peper & Salt cream & put in a shape & cover with Paste.

1 lb chicken
1 tablespoon oil
4 oz macaroni
1 ½ oz butter
1 oz plain flour (sifted)
¾ pint milk
salt (& pepper if required)
2-4 tablespoons cream
6 oz grated cheddar
1 lb ready-made puff pastry (or make your own)

1. Preheat oven to 190°C / 375°F / Gas 5.
2. Cut chicken into pieces.
3. Heat oil in a large pan and cook the chicken until lightly browned (5-10 minutes).
4. Cook macaroni in a pan of boiling water until *al dente* (stir occasionally to stop it sticking to the bottom of the pan), and drain.
5. Meanwhile, take another pan and make the white sauce. Melt the butter over a medium heat.
6. Remove the pan from the heat and stir in the sifted flour.
7. Put back on the heat and add the milk little by little, stirring vigorously all the time, until the sauce thickens. Add salt and pepper to taste.
8. Remove the sauce from the heat and add the cream.
9. Put the chicken and macaroni into a pie or casserole dish. Pour the sauce over, along with the grated cheese and stir gently to distribute evenly.
10. Roll out pastry to ¼ inch thick and make a lid for the pie.
11. Make a small hole in the centre for steam to escape. Brush with a little milk or beaten egg.
12. Bake in the centre of the oven for 30-40 minutes until pastry is risen and golden brown.

*Comments:* This makes a very rich, creamy pie that serves 4-6 people. It is delicious served with broccoli or other green vegetables.

*Cooked in:* **Electric fan oven**

*Tested by:* **Alison Baud**

1. Chafing Dish Pan.   2. Chafing Dish Stand and Lamp.   3. Double Boiler of Chafing Dish.   4. Jelly Mould.   5. Meat Slice.   6. Whisk. 7. Chafing Dish complete.   8. Colander.   9. Dutch Oven.   10. Spice Box.

# Devilling

2 teaspoonfull of Mustard 🌿 2 teaspoonfull of Anchovey Sauce
🌿 2 oz Butter

Melt Butter in baisen mix in mustard & sauce & put over meat.

2 chicken breast portions
2 oz butter
2 teasp mustard powder
2 teasp anchovy paste

1. Preheat oven to 190°C/375°F/Gas 5.
2. Cut slits into the chicken breasts to allow the sauce to penetrate, and place in a gratin dish or other shallow dish.
3. In a small saucepan melt the butter.
4. Sprinkle on the mustard powder.
5. Mix anchovy paste with butter and mustard powder to form a smooth sauce.
6. Pour over meat.
7. Cook in centre of oven for 30-35 minutes.

*Comments:* No doubt this savoury sauce is called devilling because it is so hot! Mary Jane's receipt was just for the devilling, so I had to decide what I was going to devil. I had only ever heard of devilled kidneys, but as I don't care for offal I decided to devil chicken instead. I wasn't disappointed. The chicken turned out moist and succulent, salty and spicy with a good but not overwhelming tang of anchovy. Add some cayenne if you want to make it even hotter.

It is quick and easy to make. Enjoy a glass of wine while it's cooking!

*Cooked in:* **Conventional electric oven**
*Tested by:* **Katy Jordan**

# Stewed Rabbit

Cut it in pieces & put in a jar or saucepan.  If in a jar in the oven it will take longer to cook.  Put in some stock or water & a little parsley onion peper & salt slices of Bacon & a wine glass of Port Wine after it has been stewing some time take a little fresh white stock & thicken with flour & add to the Rabbit.

2 rabbits, jointed
7 thick rashers of smoked bacon, cut into 4 chunks each
2 large red onions, sliced
1 bunch fresh parsley, roughly chopped
1 pint vegetable stock
2 large wine glasses of port
1-2 tablespoons plain flour

1. Toss meat, onions and parsley together.
2. Mix port and stock together and pour over the meat.
3. Bring to the boil on the hob and simmer (covered) for 2 hours OR for a slower cook, transfer to low oven (150°C / 300°F / Gas 2) for 4 hours.
4. Remove the rabbit, take our some liquid, mix with the flour and add back to the liquid in the pan.
5. Bring to the boil to thicken, then add the rabbit and simmer gently to re-heat.

*Comments*:  I think this would have been nicer cooked more slowly for longer, so I have suggested transferring the casserole to a slow oven. I have combined the port and stock as if you just pour the port over on its own the rabbit turns a startling shade of beetroot.

We had this as the main course at our 'Mary Jane Stratton' dinner party.  We're not used to eating rabbit very much these days, but cooked like this in port – delicious!

*Cooked on:* **Gas hob**
*Tested by:* **Kate Robinson**

# Pulled Fish

Pull any cold Fish from Bones. To 1 lb of fish add:-
½ pt of cream    🐟    1 ½ table spoonful of anchovey Sauce    🐟    a little mustard & pepper.
When it is nearly hot add to it a little flour & butter & when it is quite hot put it in your dish. Cover it with Bread Crumbs cover with butter & brown in oven.

1lb frozen white fish fillets, or fresh white fish
½ oz butter
1 tablespoon flour
½ teaspoon mustard powder
1 ½ tablespoons of anchovy paste
½ pint double cream
Salt and black pepper
Breadcrumbs, or enough mashed potato to cover the fish.

1. Preset the oven to 190°C / 375°F / Gas 5.
2. Put the frozen fish fillets into a casserole, cover and microwave these for 10 minutes at 850W, stirring several times. Reduce cooking time if you are using fresh fish.
3. Pour off the liquid and flake the fish.
4. Melt the butter in a saucepan over a gentle heat.
5. With a wooden spoon stir in the flour and mustard powder to make a paste.
6. Add the anchovy paste. The mixture will be like a lump of plasticene in consistency.
7. Add the cream a very little at a time, mixing well until it is all added and you have a creamy sauce.
8. Season with salt and pepper to taste.
9. Pour sauce over flaked fish and mix well.
10. Cover the fish with breadcrumbs, or with mashed potato. Dot with

butter.

11. **Bake on the top shelf of the oven for 15-20 minutes until the topping is brown and the dish well heated through.**

*Comments:* This gets the prize for Oddest Recipe Title in the book, and is obviously one of those dishes designed to use up leftover fish and stale bread. As very few of us these days have pounds of cooked fish lying about our kitchens, I suggest using frozen white fish. The key thing is that the fish must be cooked first. I used the microwave, but you could poach it in a little milk. I made up the dish with ready-made breadcrumbs, and it tasted very good; but I couldn't help thinking how much nicer it would have been with mashed potato topping. The anchovy and mustard sauce tastes wonderful, and the recipe was very quick and easy to do.

*Cooked in:* **Microwave; then conventional electric oven**

*Tested by:* **Katy Jordan**

*We cannot too strongly insist on the vital importance of always preserving an equable good temper amidst all the little cares and worries of domestic life. Many women may be heard to declare that men cannot realize the petty anxieties of a household. But a woman must cultivate that tact and forbearance without which no man can hope to succeed in his career. The true woman combines with mere tact that subtle sympathy which makes her the loved companion and friend alike of husband, children and all around her.* (Mrs. Beeton)

# Mrs Fearon's Fish Soufflé

Put ½ lb of cold white fish through a minceing machine, season to taste with peper & salt & a little anchovey sauce if liked, add to tablespoonfulls of finely grated breadcrumbs add the yolks of 2 eggs mix all together & moisten with milk to the consistency of thick cream lastely add the whites of the eggs beaten to a stiff froth pour into a buttered mould or baisen & steam a good hour.

8 oz good quality cooked white fish
2 medium eggs, yolks and whites
separated
1 teaspoon anchovy essence
2 tablespoons breadcrumbs
pepper & salt

1. Preheat oven to 190°C / 375°F / Gas 5.
2. Blend the fish in a blender and season to taste.
3. Add egg yolks and blend with a little milk.
4. Turn out into a bowl and add breadcrumbs.
5. Beat the egg whites until stiff.
6. Fold into the fish mixture.
7. Turn into a well-greased soufflé dish.
8. Bake for 20-25 minutes.

*Comments:* It repays using good quality fish as soufflés are delicate in flavour. Salmon would make a good alternative. Be careful with the anchovy essence as it is lethally salty.

This was good eaten cold with chilli sauce.

*Cooked in:* **Electric fan oven**
*Tested by* **Sarah Hassan**

# Tomato Soufflé

1 ½ teaspoonful of cornflower   ❧   ½ pt milk   ❧   4 oz breadcrumbs
❧   1 lb Tomatoes   ❧   3 eggs

Put the Tomatoes through a sieve make a sauce of the cornflower & milk then add to it the breadcrumbs & Tomatoes then let it go cold.  Whisk the eggs seperately when the sauce is cold add the yolks of the eggs first & then the whites mix all together pour gently into a well greased Soufflé dish & bake in a moderate oven for ½ an hour.  Cook the Tomatoes a little before putting through a sieve.
Stand the soufflé in a pan with water in the bottom to keep from burning.

1 lb tomatoes
3 teaspoons cornflour
½ pt milk
knob of butter
4 oz breadcrumbs
salt and pepper to taste
3 eggs, separated
a little grated cheddar cheese

1. Preheat oven to 190°C / 375°F / Gas 5.
2. Well grease a soufflé dish with butter, and if necessary, tie a greaseproof paper collar around it.
3. Peel (using boiling water) and deseed tomatoes.
4. In a pan, cook the tomatoes down a little to soften them.
5. In a pint jug, combine a little of the milk with the cornflour.
6. Bring the rest of the milk to the boil, pour onto the cornflour mixture, stir well, and return to the pan at a gentle heat to cook and thicken.
7. Add the butter, tomatoes and breadcrumbs.
8. Season with salt and pepper.
9. Beat the egg yolks lightly and add to the tomato mixture.
10. In a separate basin whisk the egg-whites until they are stiff and the

mixture forms soft peaks when you lift the beater out. Be careful not to over-beat them as they will collapse. With a hand mixer with balloon whisk attachment this took about 2-3 minutes.

11. Fold egg-whites into tomato mixture.

12. Pour into soufflé dish, sprinkle over the grated cheese, stand dish in a larger dish of water (bain-marie) on a baking sheet, and bake in the centre of the oven for 35-45 minutes. Test with a skewer which will come out clean if soufflé is cooked through.

*Comments:* I started with a raw weight of 1 lb of tomatoes. This went down to approximately 13 oz when peeled and deseeded. The sauce of cornflour and milk needs to be thicker than in Mary Jane's recipe, so I have doubled the cornflour used. This thicker sauce helps counteract the rather wet tomato/breadcrumb/egg mixture. I also added a little butter, and it needs a good seasoning of salt.

This is a very delicately-flavoured dish, so I also added some cheddar cheese to liven it up a little.

*Cooked in:* **Conventional electric oven**
*Tested by:* **Nicky Berry**

*Early rising contributes largely to good Household Management; she who practises this virtue reaps an ample reward both in health and prosperity. When a mistress is an early riser, it is almost certain that her house will be orderly and well managed. On the contrary, if she remain in bed till a late hour, then the servants, who, as we have observed, invariably acquire some of their mistress's characteristics, are likely to become sluggards. (Mrs. Beeton)*

# Mrs Sladen's Cheese Soufflé

1 oz Butter ✤ 1 oz Flour ✤ 1 gill of Milk ✤ ½ teaspoon of salt ✤ 3 oz grated cheese ✤ 3 yolks of eggs & 4 whites ✤ a little white & Cayenne pepper

Put in a small saucepan butter & Flour over the fire then add the milk stir till it boils & thickens take the pan off the fire & add the seasonings mix well add yolks one by one then the cheese have the whites beaten stiff & stir them in lightly pour all in a Buttered soufflé dish and bake in a quick oven over 20 minutes.

1 oz butter
1 oz plain flour
¼ pint of milk
½ teaspoon salt
pinch of Cayenne pepper
pinch of black pepper
a little ground nutmeg
4 egg whites
3 egg yolks
3 oz grated cheddar cheese (or any other hard cheese)

1. Preheat the oven to 190°C/375°F/ Gas 5.

2. Well-grease a 1½ pint soufflé dish with butter.

3. In a medium saucepan melt the butter.

4. Stir in the flour and cook over moderate heat for two minutes.

5. Gradually stir in the milk, a little at the time, until you have a smooth sauce. Cook this for 3 minutes, stirring all the time.

6. Season with salt, cayenne, and pepper, and add a little nutmeg.

7. Stir in the grated cheese.

8. Beat the egg yolks lightly to break them up, then stir them into the sauce.

9. In a separate basin whisk the egg-whites until they are stiff and the mixture forms soft peaks when you lift the beater out. Be careful not to over-beat them as they will collapse. With a hand mixer with balloon whisk attachment this took about 2-3 minutes.

10. Beat two tablespoons of the egg white into the sauce.

11. Fold in the rest of the egg white very carefully into the sauce.

12. Turn out into the soufflé dish, put dish on to a baking sheet and bake in the centre of the oven for 30-35 minutes.

13. Test with a skewer or thin knitting needle. The soufflé is cooked when the needle comes out clean.

*Comments:* Why have I always been afraid of trying soufflés? This was so easy to make, and turned out light and fluffy with a very good cheese flavour. I added some nutmeg to the ingredients, which worked well. A very nice lunch or supper dish for Wiltshire clergy and for anyone else too!

*Cooked in:* **Conventional electric oven**
*Tested by:* **Katy Jordan**

## Mrs Sladen

Sarah Victoria Eastman was born in 1861 in Southsea, Hampshire. In 1892 she married the Rev. Charles Andrew Sladen, and their daughter Evelyn Frances was born the following year. Charles was Vicar of Burton in Cheshire from 1896 to 1902, and here they kept house with just two servants, a cook and a nursemaid. They moved to Alton Barnes in 1902, and stayed there for 22 years, obviously pleased with the living and comfortable in the community.

When Mary Jane's mother was taken ill, she decided to look for work close to home, so that she could be nearby to help her father. The ideal post came up, working as cook for Rev. and Mrs. Sladen at Alton Barnes. This was just a few hundred yards away from Honeystreet and her parents' home, so she was able to visit regularly and make sure that all was well.

Mrs. Sladen contributed several recipes to Mary Jane's book. But Mrs. Sladen's new cook did not stay very long at the Rectory, for very soon she met the smart young man who called every day to deliver the post: her future husband, John Edwin Coggins.

# Mrs Sladen's Salad Dressing

2 Hard Boiled eggs ❧ 1 dessertspoonful of dry mustard
❧ 1 teaspoonfull of salt ❧ 1 teaspoonfull of Brown Sugar
❧ 1 tablespoonful Vinegar ❧ 2 tablespoonfuls of Salad
Oil ❧ ½ Cup of Cream

Yolks of 2 medium eggs, hard-
boiled
1 dessertspoon dry mustard
1 teaspoon brown sugar
1 teaspoon salt
1 tabsp cider vinegar
2 tabsp olive oil
½ cup (old-fashioned teacup!) of
cream

1. Chop egg yolks
2. Add mustard, sugar and salt, and
   fork together.

3. Slowly add vinegar, mixing to a
   paste with a fork.
4. Whisk in oil with a mixer or egg
   whisk.
5. Slowly add cream and beat until
   smooth.

*Comments*:  Very easy to make.  It
tasted quite delicious: it reminded
me of 'salad cream' but better.  It
kept in the refrigerator for two days.
It may well keep longer, but I ate it
before I could find out.

*Tested by:* **Sue Gowman**

1. Bottle Roasting Jack.   2. Mincing Knife, or Suet Chopper.   3. Meat Chopper.
4. Frying Pans.   5. Wire Meat Cover.   6. Pestle and Mortar.   7. Mincing or Sausage
Machine, with Table Clamp.   8. Double Baking Pan, with Meat Stand.   9. Drip Pan,
with Basting Ladle.   10. Bottle Jack Roasting Screen.

# Indian Toast

1 tabsp of Butter ✳ 2 eggs ✳ 1 teasp of Anchovey Paste ✳
A little Cayenne Pepper ✳ Few chopped Capers ✳ Fried bread
croutons

Put butter in a baisen & stand over a pot of boiling water when melted
stir in 2 Beaten eggs anchovey paste & Cayenne pepper & choped
capers.  Continue stiring till mixture thickens spread on croutons &
garnish & serve at once.

1 tablespoon of butter
2 eggs, beaten
1 teaspoon anchovy paste
¼ teaspoon Cayenne pepper
1 teaspoon chopped capers
Slices of toast

1. Melt butter in basin set in saucepan of boiling water.
2. Stir in beaten eggs and other ingredients.

3. Continue stirring until mixture thickens.
4. Serve on toast as a starter.  This quantity serves 2.

*Comments*: We had this as the starter at our 'Mary Jane Stratton' dinner party. Lovely taste – very rich.

*Cooked on:* **Gas hob**
*Tested by:* **Kate Robinson**

# Cheese Canapées

4 oz grated Cheese 🐝 2 oz Pounded Ham 🐝 a large Tablespoon of mixed mustard 🐝 a very little pepper & salt.

Mix into a paste with one egg spread it thickly between 2 pieces of bread cut into shapes & fry 1 minute in boiling Lard.

4 oz grated cheese
2 oz ham chopped small
1 tablespoon mustard
1 egg (whisked)
Pepper and salt to taste

1. Put all the ingredients into a basin and mix.
2. Cut the crusts off two slices of bread, and sandwich together with some of the mixture.
3. Heat some oil in frying pan, and fry sandwich on each side for about a minute (no more).
4. Repeat until mixture is all used up. This quantity made 5 rounds.

*Comments*: Eat immediately – this won't be a problem! Fantastic. Delicious. Top marks.

*Cooked on*: **Gas hob**
*Tested by*: **Linda Jordan**

*The functions of the mistress of a house resemble those of the general of an army or the manager of a great business concern. Her spirit will be seen in the whole establishment, and if she performs her duties well and intelligently, her domestics will usually follow in her path. (Mrs. Beeton)*

# 2

# Baked Puddings

❧

I n baking as in all other methods of cookery the surrounding air may be many degrees hotter than boiling water, but the food is not appreciably hotter until it has lost water by evaporation, after which it may readily burn. The hot air of the oven is greedy of water, and evaporation is great, so that ordinary baking (i.e. just to shut the food into a hot-air chamber) is not suited for anything that needs moist heat…

To test the heat of an oven special thermometers are made… [Alternatively] the heat may be tested with a sheet of writing paper, which curls up brown in a pastry oven, or with flour, which takes every shade from coffee colour to black, when sprinkled on the floor of the oven. Experienced cooks test very accurately with the hand.

*Mrs. Beeton (1907), p.114.*

Puddings of all kinds are by far the most common recipes in Mary Jane's receipt-book: she collected well over one hundred altogether. I have not included them all here, but there are still so many that I felt it would be helpful to divide them into three sections: baked puddings, steamed or boiled puddings, and set desserts. There are some old favourites here, and some you will not have met before.

The baked puddings include several of what I have come to think of as Mary Jane's 'topographical recipes', those named after places, as in 'Derbyshire pudding'.   Occasionally I can make sense of these, when a place seems particularly associated with one of the ingredients.   Devonshire pudding contains apples, which is fair enough, but what has Nassau to do with orange marmalade?  Is Derbyshire pudding supposed to be a Bakewell pie, and if so, will Bakewell people be offended?

# Nassaw Pudding

Beat 4 oz Butter to a cream with 4 oz Sugar add 3 eggs add lastly 2 table spoonfull of Orange Marmalade beat well & pour in a Buttered Pie dish & bake.

4 oz butter
4 oz granulated sugar
3 large eggs, whisked lightly
together
2 tablespoons of good thick orange
marmalade, preferably home-made

1. Preheat the oven to 170°C / 325°F / Gas 3.
2. Grease a shallow casserole dish.
3. Beat the butter to a cream.
4. Add the sugar and beat again to a cream.
5. Beat in the eggs, a little at a time.
6. Stir in the marmalade.
7. Turn out into the casserole dish.
8. Bake in the top of the oven for 40 minutes.
9. Serve at once.   Serves 2.

*Comments*: This makes a light, eggy sponge with an orange syrup. It's important to use good quality thick marmalade, so that you don't get too much syrup. You must eat it immediately, as it doesn't keep. This probably won't be a problem!   It tastes absolutely gorgeous.

*Cooked in:* **Conventional electric oven**
*Tested by:* **Katy Jordan**

# Marmalade Pudding

Take a Pie Dish three parts full with sliced bread & Butter & put a thick coating of Marmalade between each layer.  Fill up the dish with good custard & let it stand for 1 hr after which bake the Pudding in a moderate oven till the custard is quite set & be carefull not to let the Pudding boil.

6 slices of stale white bread
½ jar marmalade – home-made
Seville is best
2 oz butter
1 pt milk
2 eggs

1.  Preheat oven to 170°C / 325°F / Gas 3.
2.  Butter bread and spread thickly with marmalade.
3.  Cut into quarters and place in a buttered pie dish.
4.  Beat eggs with milk and strain this over bread.
5.  Leave for one hour.
6.  Bake in oven for 1 hour; OR Cook for 1 hour in main oven of Aga with plain shelf above

*Comments:* I would stress that it's important to use slightly stale bread. Mine was too fresh, and leaving the pudding for 1 hour to stand made it a bit too soggy.  Drier bread would work much better.  To save time you could make this with ready-made custard.

*Cooked in:* **Aga**
*Tested by:* **Sue Chadwick**

# Orange Pudding

Any thick slices of any kind of sweet cake in a deep pie dish. Over this pour hot custard made from 3 eggs, a pt of milk, half a teacup of sugar, and the Grated rind of quarter of a Lemon. Do this several hours before the dish is to be served just before serving put a layer of sliced oranges over the cake have the whites of the eggs beaten to a stiff froth with 2 tablespoonful of sugar add a few drops of Lemon juice & put over the fruit, put into a oven & brown.

Madeira cake slices
2 oranges, sliced

*For custard:*
3 eggs
2 oz caster sugar
1 pt milk
2 oz caster sugar
1 teaspoon cornflour

*For meringue:*
1 lemon
2 egg whites

1. Preheat the oven to 200°C / 400°F / Gas 6.
2. Cover the base of a deep pie dish with the madeira cake slices.

3. *Make the custard:* blend together the eggs, caster sugar, cornflour and grated rind of half the lemon. Heat the milk until just about to simmer, pour milk over egg mixture and stir well, then return to pan. Heat very gently until mixture thickens.
4. Pour custard into cold bowl to prevent further cooking, and leave to cool.
5. Pour cooled custard onto the cake slices.
6. Arrange the orange slices on top of the custard.
7. *Make the meringue:* whisk egg whites until they are stiff. Add caster sugar, and whisk again until stiff. Fold in 1 teaspoon lemon juice.

8. **Cook in oven for 10 minutes, to brown the meringue.**
9. **Eat cold.**

*Comments:* This makes a very moist pudding with a delicate flavour.

Keep it in the fridge and eat within a couple of days.

*Cooked in:* **Gas oven**
*Tested by:* **Verity Smith**

# Derbyshire Pudding

Boil 2 tablespoonfulls of flour in a pt of New Milk until it is thick then let it cool. Soften ¼ lb Butter & beat with a fork. Add ½ a lb of Sifted Sugar, the Yolks of 5 eggs & whites of 2 eggs beat well, the rind of a Lemon mix all together. Line a dish with pastry. Bake about ¾ of an hour in a moderate oven when ready cover the top well over with Apricot Jam. Beat the whites of eggs & pile over the top. Bake 5 minutes to brown.

1 pint whole milk
2 tablespoons plain flour
4 oz unsalted butter
8 oz caster sugar
Zest of 1 lemon (unwaxed)
5 eggs
Short-crust pastry to line 20/25cm flan dish OR a shop-bought unsweetened short-crust pastry case

❧

1. Preset oven to 190°C / 375°F / Gas 5.
2. Mix flour with milk in a pan and bring to boil, whisking all the time. Boil for a few minutes until milk thickens. Put aside to cool.
3. Line a flan dish with unsweetened short-crust pastry and bake blind OR use a shop-bought pastry case.
4. Beat butter, sugar, lemon zest and 5 egg yolks and 2 egg whites together until well combined.
5. Pour into pastry case and bake in oven for 45 minutes.
6. Whisk remaining 3 egg whites until they form stiff peaks, then pile on flan.
7. Return to oven and bake for 5-10 mins until golden brown.

*Comments:* The whisked egg does not really behave like meringue in that it shrinks from the sides and is more chewy, but still nice.

The lemon custard has a pleasant grainy texture and the lemon flavour is quite strong.

It keeps well for a couple of days (but not so good at surviving unbashed up the M6!)

I made the pudding with a shop-bought sweet shortcrust pastry case which I think was overall too sweet, hence the recommendation for unsweetened pastry. However my tasters really liked it as it was.

*Cooked in:* **Conventional electric oven**
*Tested by:* **Isobel Stark**

## At a Devizes school

ary Jane's first experience of working life was at one of the schools in Devizes. There were several schools in the town at the time, but it seems most likely that she was employed at the Boys' Elementary School in Maryport street. Here the headmaster was Horatio Whitting, the younger brother of her old headmaster at Woodborough.[1] Since the family of his good pupil Mary Jane Stratton could not afford to keep her on at school as a Monitor, Ernest Whitting could at least recommend her to his brother as a good and reliable servant.

> Elementary Schools.
>
> Boys', Maryport street, built in 1882, for 210 children; average attendance, 140; Horatio Whitting, master
>
> Girls', Sheep street, erected for 150 children; average attendance, 143; Miss Eva Cross, mistress
>
> Infants', Sheep street, built for 200 children; average attendance, 115; Miss Maria Upham, mistress
>
> St. Peter's, built in 1870 & enlarged in 1893, for 265 children; average attendance, 221; S. E. White, master; Miss Ada Smith, infants' mistress & Miss Theresa E. Carr, girls' mistress
>
> Southbroom, The Green, established in 1834, & largely rebuilt in 1894, at a cost of about £500, for 165 boys, 134 girls & 160 infants; average attendance, 144 boys, 140 girls & 130 infants; George French Smith, master; Miss Emma Seabright, mistress; Mrs. Alice Webb, infants' mistress
>
> Catholic (Middle Class School), conducted by the Sisters of St. Joseph
>
> Catholic, St. Joseph's place; accommodation, 160; average attendance, 133; conducted by the Sisters of St. Joseph

The first task of the day for the kitchen-maid was always to light the range, and Mary Jane used to recount how her parsimonious employer would allow her just six sticks of kindling and one sheet of newspaper to light the fire in the morning!

[1] *Kelly's Directory of Wiltshire* (1903). London: Kelly's Directories, p.88

# Princess Amelia's Puddings

> Take 5 large Apples prepare as for sauce & add while hot 2 oz Butter & when cold 2 eggs well beaten a few breadcrumbs a little Nutmeg & sugar mix alltogether & bake in little cups turn them out sift Sugar over & serve.

2 or 3 lbs cooking apples
2 oz butter
2 eggs, beaten
a handful of breadcrumbs
2 oz caster sugar
a little grated nutmeg
icing sugar

1. Preheat oven to 180°C / 350°F / Gas 4.
2. Peel and slice apples, and put into a saucepan with a little water. Simmer until soft.
3. Add the butter, and stir well.
4. Allow the mixture to cool right down.
5. Add the eggs, breadcrumbs, sugar, and nutmeg.
6. Put mixture into 6 greased dariole moulds or individual greased cups.
7. Bake in the oven for 30-45 minutes.
8. Remove from oven, turn out, sift icing sugar over them and serve hot.

*Comments:* I judged 'five large apples' to be about 2 lbs, but perhaps I should have used nearer 3 lbs. With the quantities I used, this pudding seemed rather bland, and more apples might sharpen the flavour. I think this could be a very tasty pudding, especially served with home-made custard.

*Cooked in:* **Gas oven**
*Tested by:* **Sheila Page**

# Devonshire Pudding

Line a Pie dish with apricot jam and upon this place a layer of apples cut in rings put a pt of milk on the fire & when boiling add 2 oz breadcrumbs allow it to thicken then sweeten to taste add 2 eggs well beaten & flavour with any kind of essence. Pour this over the apples & bake in a moderate oven from 15 to 20 minutes.

2 tablespoons apricot jam (good quality or home-made)
1 large cooking apple
1 pint whole milk
1 tablespoon cornflour
2 oz breadcrumbs
2 eggs, yolks and whites separated
½ teasp vanilla essence

1. Preset oven to 180°C/350°F/Gas 4.
2. Cover the base of a pie dish or shallow casserole with a thick layer of apricot jam.
3. Cover the jam with a layer of apple, cut in discs.
4. Heat the milk in a pan, but reserve a little in a pint jug and mix this smoothly with the cornflour.
5. When the milk is hot, pour it on to the cornflour paste and stir well, then return to the pan and keep on the heat.
6. Add the breadcrumbs, and stir until the sauce thickens.
7. Add the sugar, beaten eggs and vanilla essence, and mix it all well together.
8. Pour the sauce over the apples and bake for 20 minutes.
9. Serve cold.

*Comments:* This is a good mixture of flavours, with the sharpness of the apples sweetened by the jam and vanilla sauce. The breadcrumbs plus the cornflour thicken the sauce and make this quite a substantial pudding. I used apricot jam with brandy, which certainly added interest! Make sure you use good quality thick jam or the pudding will be too runny.

*Cooked in:* **Conventional electric oven**
*Tested by:* **Katy Jordan**

# Sultana Pudding

Take 2 ½ oz or 5 tablespoonfull of Cornflower
2 pts or 3 large breakfast cups of milk
Perpare as for B. Mange before boiling add 2 yolks of eggs & 1 ½ oz
sugar add sultanas.  Pour into a Pie dish allow to cool & bake in a
gentile oven till brown on top.  Can leave out eggs.

2 ½ oz cornflour
1 ½ oz sugar
2 pints full-fat milk
Yolks of 2 eggs
1 teaspoon vanilla essence
1 ½ oz sultanas

1. Preheat oven to 150°C / 300°F / Gas 2.
2. Mix together the cornflour and sugar in a 2 pint jug, and mix with enough milk to make a smooth paste.
3. Heat the rest of the milk in a large saucepan until almost at boiling point.
4. Pour milk on to the cornflour paste and mix well.
5. Return sauce to the pan but don't put it back on the heat yet.
6. Beat the egg-yolks lightly together and add this to the sauce.
7. Add the vanilla essence, and stir the sauce well.
8. Turn the heat down to very low and bring the sauce very slowly to the boil, stirring often so that it does not burn.
9. When the sauce thickens, add the sultanas, and continue cooking at a gentle simmer for 1-2 minutes, to ensure the sauce is properly cooked.
10. Remove from heat, pour into a 2-pint dish, and cool slightly.
11. Bake in the centre of the oven for about 30 minutes until the pudding is brown on top.

*Comments:*  Intensive testing has revealed that this pudding is best prepared in advance and eaten cold, as then it sets like a blancmange and has a much more pleasing texture. However, it's pretty good hot too. The sultanas swell up during cooking and the flavour combines well with vanilla essence, but you could try it with other flavourings.

Enjoyed during the testing stage by adults and children alike.

*Cooked on:* **Electric hob**
*Tested by:* **Katy Jordan**

1. Household Weighing Machine.    2. Oval Boiling Pot.    3. Turbot Kettle.
4. Copper Preserving-pan.    5. Fish Kettle.    6. Bain Marie Pans.    7. Iron Stockpot with Tap.    8. Saucepan and Steamer.    9. Steak Tongs.    10. Fish Slice.

# Gooseberry & Rhubarb Turnovers

Stew ½ bundle of Rhubarb with sugar, drain & Rub through a Sieve.
Make puff paste roll & cut into squares. Spread this with the pulp
which should be rather thick, on half of this pile some green
Gooseberries. Sprinke with Sugar & a little cinamon. Double paste
over & bake.

1 lb rhubarb
¾ pint water
4 oz sugar, or to taste
1lb puff pastry
8 oz fresh gooseberries; or a can of
gooseberries, drained.
Sugar to sprinkle
Cinnamon

1. Preset oven to 230°C / 450°F / Gas 8.
2. Grease a baking sheet.
3. Stew rhubarb in water with sugar until tender.
4. Drain liquid from rhubarb and allow fruit to cool.
5. Liquidise fruit to make a pulp.
6. Roll out the puff pastry evenly into a square abour ¼ inch thick, and cut into four squares.
7. Spread each square thickly with rhubarb pulp.
8. Near one corner of each square put a few gooseberries.
9. Sprinkle fruit with sugar and cinnamon.
10. Double pastry over to make four triangular turnovers and pinch the corners together to hold them firm. Leave the sides open so that the fruit is visible.
11. Cut 2 vents in the folded edge of each pastry.
12. Brush with milk to glaze.
13. Bake in top half of oven for 15-20 minutes until risen and golden brown.

*Comments:* Serve hot or cold with cream or custard. This makes six turnovers, or four really substantial ones.

    This really was a case of 'how to cheat at cookery'. I used the rhubarb pulp left over from the Rhubarb sponge recipe (p.57), with canned gooseberries and readymade puff pastry. All I had to do was put the turnovers together. Later I tried them with fresh gooseberries, but there was little difference between them. This recipe comes highly recommended. It looks impressive, and is really delicious, hot or cold.

*Cooked in:* **Conventional electric oven**
*Tested by:* **Katy Jordan**

*Engaging servants is one of the most important duties the mistress is called upon to perform. One of the commonest ways of procuring servants is to answer advertisements or to insert a notice, setting forth what kind of servant is required... There are many respectable registry-offices, where good servants may be hired. A good plan is for the mistress to tell friends and acquaintances of the vacant place. A lady whose general relations with her domestics are friendly, and fairly permanent, will seldom need to employ any of these methods. Suitable applicants will soon present themselves to fill the vacant places, generally friends of the domestic who is obliged to leave.* (Mrs. Beeton)

# 3

# Boiled or Steamed Puddings

❧

Success in preparing dishes of this class depends more on suitable proportions, manipulation, and the proper application of heat than on the materials themselves, which are usually of a simple character.

Boiled puddings: To ensure perfect cooking, the following rules, which apply equally to rich or plain, large or small puddings, must be observed.

1. The mould or basin must be perfectly dry and well coated with butter or fat.
2. The pudding must completely fill the mould or basin.
3. A scalded and floured cloth should be tied securely over the top of the basin.
4. The water must be boiling rapidly when the pudding is put in.
5. The water must completely cover the pudding, and be deep enough to float those boiled in cloths, otherwise a plate or saucer must be placed at the bottom of the pan.
6. As the water boils away, boiling water must be added.
7. The pudding must stand a few minutes before being turned out, in order that some of the steam may escape, and thus cause the pudding to shrink and be less liable to break.

Steamed puddings: Puddings steamed over water are lighter than when immersed in it, but they cook more slowly. A quicker method, and one that gives practically the same results, is to stand the pudding in a saucepan containing boiling water to about half the depth of the mould or basin, the surrounding water being frequently replenished with more boiling water. A pudding to be steamed should not more than three-quarters fill the basin; and two folds of paper, made waterproof by being rubbed with butter or fat, should cover the top instead of a cloth, which prevents the pudding rising.

*Mrs Beeton 1907, pp.913-4*

These are Mrs Beeton's instructions for boiling and steaming the kind of puddings you will find in this chapter. Most testers chose the half-steamed-half-boiled method of cooking that Mrs. Beeton suggests above as a quicker method of steaming. Nowadays we might add pressure cooking and micro-waving to the methods we can use successfully to cook a pudding.

These substantial puddings are out of fashion now, and I certainly would not recommend them as daily fare. But as a warming pud for cold winter days, or for Sunday lunch with all the family, they are very enjoyable and a real taste of less calorie-conscious times.

# Chocolate Pudding

½ lb Chocolate  ✢  2 eggs  ✢  ¼ rusks  ✢  2 oz sugar

Boil chocolate with lump sugar till disolved add yolks of eggs & a little butter when cold add the stiffley beaten whites line a baisen with rusks & steam.

3 oz sponge fingers
8 oz plain chocolate
2 oz sugar
knob of butter
2 eggs, separated yolks and whites

1. Lightly grease a 1 pint basin and line it with sponge fingers, sugar side to the basin.
2. Melt the chocolate with the sugar in a bowl set over a saucepan of boiling water.
3. When dissolved, add butter and egg yolks, mixing well.
4. Set aside to cool.
5. Beat the egg whites to form stiff peaks, and fold into the cooled chocolate mixture.
6. Pour the mousse into the lined basin, cover with pleated greased tinfoil and tie down.
7. Steam in a pressure cooker for 5 minutes with no weight, then 15 minutes at low pressure.
8. Turn out carefully onto a serving plate and eat hot.

*Comments:* The most difficult part was lining the basin with sponge fingers – they didn't want to stay where they were put! The kitchen fills with a delectable chocolaty aroma while it's cooking. What you get is a dark chocolate mousse inside a sponge case, rich and filling. It must surely count as the Edwardian equivalent of Death By Chocolate.

Leftovers in the fridge set hard, but 30 seconds per portion in the microwave turns it back into hot foamy chocolate mousse again.

*Cooked in:* **Pressure cooker**
*Tested by:* **Katy Jordan**

# Iris Pudding

2 oz Butter    🦅    2 ½ oz Flour    🦅    ¼ teaspoonful of Bkg Powder
🦅    1 tea spoon Chocolate    🦅    2 oz Sugar    🦅    1 egg    🦅    a
little milk    🦅    essence of Vanellea

Steam 1 hr.

2 oz butter
2 oz sugar
1 egg, lightly beaten
2 ½ oz plain flour
¼ teaspoon baking powder
1 teaspoon cocoa
Vanilla essence to taste
a little milk

1. Cream butter and sugar.
2. Beat in egg.
3. Stir in sifted dry ingredients.
4. Add vanilla and a little milk to

make a soft dough.
5. Turn into a greased 1 pint basin
   and steam or boil for one hour.

*Comments:*  This is delicious.  Very
light taste.  It would however be
improved with a sauce, custard or a
base of raspberry jam.
    This is a small pudding –
serves 2-3.

*Cooked in:* **Conventional electric oven**
*Tested by:*  **Christine Clist and Rachel-**
    **Mary Perry**

🦅   *Cleanliness is quite indispensable to Health, and must be studied
both in regard to the person and the house, and all that it contains.  Cold
or tepid baths should be employed every morning.*  (Mrs. Beeton) 🦅

# Marmalade Pudding

¼ lb Flour 🌿 ¼ lb Sugar 🌿 ¼ Chopped Suet 🌿 ¼
Breadcrumbs 🌿 ¼ Marmalade 🌿 ¼ pt Milk 🌿 pinch of
Salt 🌿 ½ Teaspoonfull of Baking Powder

Mix dry Ingredients together then add beaten eggs & marmalade. Put
in Greased baisen & steam for 2 hours.

2 oz Self Raising flour
2 oz caster sugar
2 oz suet
2 oz brown breadcrumbs
pinch salt
2 oz thick-cut marmalade,
preferably home-made
3 fl oz milk
1 egg

1. Mix the dry ingredients together.
2. Beat the egg, and mix with the milk.
3. Add the marmalade and the egg and milk mixture to the dry ingredients, and mix well together.
4. Put into a greased 1½ pint basin, and cover with a layer of greased greaseproof paper and tinfoil.
5. Bring to the boil, simmer for ½ hour and steam for 2 hours.
6. Serve with custard.

*Comments:* Very popular – everyone asked for seconds including our Chinese and Japanese visitors. But the greatest fan is definitely Simon (aged 9 months) who couldn't get enough of it. It is nice but nondescript if made with thin cut marmalade. It's a lovely light texture for a suet pudding. The above list is for a half size pudding, but I'll probably have to make a full size one from now on (mainly to feed the baby ... ) Leftovers keep quite well, so it could probably be made in advance and reheated.

*Cooked on:* **Aga**
*Tested by* **Helen Williams**

# Ashfield Pudding

½ lb Flour    🐝    2 oz Butter    🐝    ¼ lb Castor Sugar    🐝    1 teaspoonfull of Baking Powder    🐝    1 egg    🐝    1 gill of milk

Rub the Butter in flour, the sugar & baking powder.  Mix well with the egg & milk.  Butter a baisen put a tablespoonfull of jam at the bottom & steam for 2 hours.

8 oz plain flour
1 teaspoon baking powder
2 oz butter
4 oz caster sugar
1 egg
¼ pt milk
2 tablespoons jam

1. Well butter a 2-pint pudding basin.
2. In a large mixing bowl, sift together the flour and baking powder.
3. Rub in the butter.
4. Sift the sugar and stir in well.
5. Lightly beat the egg and with a wooden spoon stir into the mixture.
6. Stir in the milk a little at a time to make a smooth mixture.
7. Put the jam into the bottom of the buttered pudding basin.
8. Turn the mixture out into the basin.
9. Microwave at 850W for 4 minutes.  Leave to stand for 5 minutes to finish cooking.  Test with a fine skewer, and if not cooked through, microwave a further 30 seconds or as necessary.
10. Serve immediately with hot custard.

*Comments:*  If you cook it in the microwave, this is a very quick and easy pudding to make.  You can, of course, steam it as Mary Jane would have done, and I think it would be better for it.  It would certainly dry out less quickly if you do.  But being a busy working woman, I decided to use the microwave.  Ideally, if you microwave it, then eat it all at once to experience it at its best (you will need help with this!).

I recommend that for the jam you use Mary Jane's rhubarb and ginger jam (see p.123). It is less sweet than commercial jams, and combines well with the sponge. This is a substantial pudding, and you will definitely need to eat it with custard to moisten it.

*Cooked using:* **Microwave (850W)**
*Tested by:* **Katy Jordan**

# Blackberry Pudding

8 oz Flour ❧ 2 oz Butter ❧ 2 oz Castor Sugar ❧ ½
teaspoonful carbonate of Soda ❧ ½ teaspoonful salt ❧ 1 lb ripe
Blackberries ❧ 1 small teacup of Golden Syrup warmed & mixed
with the other ingredients.

Pour into a Buttered mould & steam for 3 hrs.  Serve with cream or sauce.

8 oz plain flour
½ teaspoon bicarbonate of soda
2 oz butter
2 oz caster sugar
8 oz blackberries
¼ mug of golden syrup

1. Rub butter into flour and bicarbonate of soda.
2. Stir in sugar and blackberries and then finally golden syrup and mix well.
3. Pour into a greased basin and cover leaving room for mixture to expand.
4. Steam for 3 hours.

*Comments:* Made with the quantities Mary Jane gives, the mix was cooked but the combination of sticky syrup and such a large quantity of blackberries meant the pudding did not hold its shape when turned out. So I feel it needs to be made with half the quantities Mary Jane gives for blackberries and syrup. We ate it with ice cream and it was quite palatable although very sticky – my amended quantities above should solve the stickiness problem.

*Cooked in:* **Steamer**
*Tested by:* **Sue Chadwick**

# Paradise Pudding

2 eggs  ❧  3 apples  ❧  ¼ lb of breadcrumbs  ❧  3 oz sugar
❧  2 oz Currents  ❧  salt & grated nutmeg to taste.  ❧  The
rind of ½ a Lemon grated  ❧  ½ a Wine Glass of Brandy

Pare & mince the apples mix with the dry Ingredients beat up the eggs
moisten the mixture with them stir in the brandy & boil 2 hrs.

1 lb cooking apples
4 oz breadcrumbs
3 oz caster sugar
2 oz raisins
Grated rind of half a lemon
Salt and nutmeg to taste
2 eggs
1 ½ fl oz brandy

❧

1. Put on steamer, with base half-filled with water; or half-fill a large saucepan. Heat so that the water is boiling by the time the pudding is made.
2. Peel and core apples, and put through a mincer or food processor to chop fine.
3. Put apple pulp, breadcrumbs, sugar, raisins, lemon rind, salt and grated nutmeg into a large bowl and mix thoroughly.
4. Beat eggs and add to mixture.
5. Add brandy and stir well.
6. Well grease a 1½ pint pudding basin and put in mixture. It should be only two-thirds full. Cover with a double layer of greaseproof paper or foil to prevent the water getting in.
7. Place pudding in steamer or saucepan of water. Steam or boil for 2 hours. Remember to top up the water, as it boils away quite quickly.

*Comments:* I followed Mary Jane's quantities (3 cooking apples are about 1 lb) but used raisins rather than currants. I used foil to cover the pudding.

This pudding lived up to its name – it was delicious. Eat it immediately while it's nice and hot. I'm sure cream, custard or ice cream would be an excellent accompaniment.

*Cooked on:* **Gas hob**

*Tested by:* **Sheila Page**

# Bachelor's Pudding

4 oz Breadcrumbs 🐝 4 oz Currents 🐝 4 oz apples 🐝 2 oz sugar 🐝 2 or 3 eggs 🐝 A few drops of lemon essence 🐝 A little grated nutmeg.

Peel core and mince the apples which must be 4 oz. Add the currents bread and sugar and the well beaten eggs and boil 3 hours.

4 oz prepared apple (peeled, cored and chopped)
4 oz breadcrumbs
4 oz currants
2 oz sugar
3 medium eggs, beaten well
1 tablespoon of Jif lemon
1 teaspoon of grated nutmeg.

1. Butter a pudding basin with a capacity of at least 2½ pints.
2. In a large bowl put all the ingredients and mix well together.
3. Turn mixture into the prepared basin and cover with greased & pleated tinfoil or greaseproof paper.
4. Stand basin in a saucepan of boiling water and cook for 3 hours.

*Comments:* The pudding is very simple to make, and comes out a lovely golden colour flecked with plumped up currants. Pick a bowl with room for the mixture to rise as it cooks. We chose a 2-pint bowl and it was only just big enough.

It is a moist appley sort of bread and butter pudding. Definitely one to be made again. Looks a gem for cooler days, eaten with proper custard, or cream, or a good vanilla or clotted cream ice cream – and the chance for a long snooze afterwards.

*Cooked on:* **Rayburn hob**
*Tested by:* **Helena Cave-Penney**

# Fig Pudding

¾ lb brown breadcrumbs  ✽  6 oz Suet  ✽  ½ lb Figs chopped
✽  4 oz Sugar  ✽  1 egg  ✽  A Grate of Nutmeg & Lemon rind.

Mix altogether & moisten with milk & boil 3 hours.

12 oz breadcrumbs
6 oz vegetable suet
8 oz dried figs, chopped
4 oz sugar
1 egg
Juice and rind of one lemon
Grated nutmeg

1. Grease a 1 pint pudding basin.
2. Mix all the ingredients together really well.
3. Turn out into pudding basin, and cover with layers of greaseproof paper and foil, or a pudding cloth.
4. Boil the pudding in a large pan of boiling water for 3 hours, checking regularly and adding boiling water so that the pan does not boil dry.

*Comments:* The pudding is mild in taste, and the lemon was more noticeable when served hot. It is like a fig cake when cold and excellent with ice cream. You can taste the fat of the suet, but it is probably all needed for the binding. I suggest adding the juice of the lemon as well as the lemon rind to give a nice tang to the flavour.

Good for using up left-over bread and dried figs at Christmas.

*Cooked in:* **Rayburn**
*Tested by:* **Helena Cave-Penney**

# Severn Cup Pudding

1 cup of flour ❧ 1 of breadcrumbs ❧ 1 of sugar ❧ 1 of suet ❧ 1 of jam ❧ 1 of milk ❧ 1 of sultanas ❧ 1 teaspoonful of Baking Powder

Steam for 3 hours.

1 cup Self-Raising flour
1 cup breadcrumbs
1 cup sugar
1 cup margarine (or suet)
1 cup good thick apricot jam,
preferably home-made
1 cup milk
1 cup sultanas
1 teasp baking powder

❧❧❧

1. Mix all ingredients together.
2. Turn into a greased pudding basin large enough for the mixture to no more than two-thirds fill the basin. This allows for the pudding to rise.
3. Cover with two sheets of greased foil, fastened securely to prevent water getting in during cooking.
4. Put 1½ pints of water into a pressure cooker.
5. Steam the pudding in the pressure cooker without a weight for 15 minutes, then cook at 5 lb pressure for 25 minutes.

*Comments:* A very moist, quite heavy pudding. The cup of jam seemed to make it very wet and rather sloppy. Using a very good quality commercial or a home-made jam with more fruit than syrup would reduce the wetness. Or you could pour the jam into the bottom of the basin before adding the rest of the mixture, so that when turned out the jam runs down over the cooked sponge.

*Cooked in:* **Pressure cooker**
*Tested by:* **Linda Jordan**

# Mrs Loveredge's Christmas Pudding

1 ½ Raisens   🌿   1 ½ Currents   🌿   1 ½ sugar   🌿   ¾ flour   🌿
¾ breadcrumbs   🌿   6 oz Candid Peel   🌿   1 ½ suet   🌿   7 or 8
eggs   🌿   a few chopped almonds   🌿   1 ½ glass of wine   🌿   1
glass of Brandy   🌿   a little salt

Make in 3 Puddings

1 lb raisins
1 lb currants
1 glass wine
⅔  glass brandy
1 lb margarine OR 1 lb suet
1 lb light brown sugar
10 oz Self-Raising flour
Pinch of salt
8 oz breadcrumbs
4 oz candied peel
A few chopped almonds
5 large eggs or 6 medium

❧

1. Soak raisins and currants in brandy and wine overnight.
2. Cream the butter and sugar together.
3. Add the other ingredients: flour, salt, breadcrumbs, peel, nuts and eggs, and mix well together until it is all thoroughly combined.
4. Divide the mixture equally into two pudding basins.
5. Steam in pressure cooker for 30 minutes without weights; then for 2 hours at 15 lb pressure.
6. This quantity makes two 2-pint puddings.

*Comments:*  The quantities were huge, so I'm very glad I reduced them by one-third.  I used light brown sugar, but you could use dark brown if you wanted a darker pudding.

   Taste-tested on Christmas Day 2002 by the entire Jordan family. Unanimous verdict: a really superb

pudding, deliciously alcoholic. *Cooked in:* **Pressure cooker**
Highly recommended. *Tested by:* **Linda Jordan**

We don't know who you were, Mrs Loveredge, but thank you!

## Lady Jemima Johnson

Among the family photographs, there is a postcard of Woodborough church, addressed to Miss M. Stratton, *The Hill*, Upton-on-Severn, Worcestershire. This single clue indicates that at some point in her career, Mary Jane must have worked at *The Hill*, once the dower house of a large estate nearby, and at that time residence of Lady Jemima Johnson.

Lady Jemima was born Jemima Anne Frances Martin, the daughter of Rev. George Martin, Chancellor of the Diocese of Exeter. In 1860 she married Charles Cooper Johnson, an officer of the Indian Army, and 6th son of Sir Henry Allen Johnson, 2nd Baronet. During the Indian Mutiny, Charles served under Lord Clyde at the siege of Lucknow, and he was Quartermaster-General of the Army in India during the Afghan Campaign from 1878-80. In 1889 he was promoted to Lieutenant-General.

We can judge the size of their household from the 1881 census information, which shows that Colonel Sir Charles Johnson (as he was at that stage of his career), his wife Jemima, their 9-year old son Allen and Lady Jemima's two unmarried sisters were living at *The Hill* with a staff of nine indoor servants. At that period, the family needed the services of a housekeeper, lady's maid, cook, parlour maid, housemaid, under-housemaid, kitchen-maid and footman. There must also have been several outside staff: Major F.S. Jewell Maurice, who bought *The Hill* from Lady Johnson in 1912, kept a staff of three gardeners to maintain the extensive gardens. General Sir Charles died in 1905, and it is possible that the household was not quite so large by the time Mary Jane worked there. Like Lady Malcolm, Lady Jemima may have had to reduce her household somewhat to manage on a reduced income.

How did Mary Jane come to be working in Worcestershire? Servants answered advertisements for jobs, of course, but many employers preferred to take on staff on personal recommendation from friends and acquaintances. Both Wilhelmina Malcolm and Jemima Johnson were clergyman's daughters from Devon, and both were wives of officers of the Army in India. They must have known each other, and it is quite possible that Lady Johnson employed Mary Jane as cook on the recommendation of her friend Lady Malcolm.

As cook, Mary Jane would have been one of the more privileged members of staff, allowed to rise as late as 7 a.m., perhaps even woken with a cup of tea brought her by the kitchen-maid. She had a comfortable room in

*The Hill, Upton on Severn*

the servants' wing of the house, which adjoined the kitchen and servants' hall. No doubt she worked very hard in the kitchen that was her domain, but when she looked out from *The Hill* over to Bredon hill across the valley, or visited the pleasant little town of Upton-on-Severn, she must have felt she could be working in far worse places. Perhaps it was here at Upton-on-Severn that Mary Jane collected the pudding recipe that calls for seven cups of ingredients. Why else would she call it *Severn* Cup Pudding?

# 4

# Set Desserts

❧

This branch of cookery affords almost unlimited scope for display of artistic taste. Each section of the mould must be decorated separately, and the decoration fixed firmly by means of a little cold jelly, which must be allowed to set before changing the position of the mould. For this reason the process is a slow one unless the mould meanwhile rests upon and is surrounded by ice. Without this aid the task is almost an impossible one in hot weather.

*Mrs Beeton (1907), p. 985*

Here Mrs Beeton is referring to the decorated 'shapes' – jellies, creams, solid custards and so on – which were set in fancy moulds, and at their most complicated were decorated with jellied fruits or set in different-coloured layers. Forget your childhood memories of jelly-and-ice-cream: these are truly aristocratic desserts.

Mary Jane collected a number of different jellies and creams, none of which are difficult or time-consuming to prepare, especially in these days of refrigerators. These desserts can be set in plain dishes or bowls, but a real jelly-mould makes them much more attractive.

*Where to find jelly-moulds*
Specialist kitchen shops stock modern metal and plastic moulds. I bought a beautiful reproduction Victorian porcelain mould in the gift-shop of one of our large country houses. Seek out real old porcelain or glass moulds in antique and junk shops, car boot sales, internet sites like *E-Bay*, or the store cupboards of elderly relatives.

*How to turn out a jelly (or other set dessert)*
Mrs Beeton and Sheila Page (who kindly loaned me two of her collection of antique jelly-moulds) both give the same advice:-
1. Rinse the mould with cold water before pouring in the jelly.
2. When it is set, use your fingertips to ease the jelly gently away from the sides of the mould.
3. Then plunge the mould into a bowl of hot water for 30 seconds. Don't soak it for longer, or the moulded surface of the jelly will start to melt and lose definition.
4. Place a plate over the mould, turn them over together, and use a sharp up-down movement to turn out the jelly.

*Cabinet Pudding*

# Cabinet Pudding

Butter a mould oramenent with strips of Angelica & Cherries now fill the mould 3 parts full with Sponge Cakes.  Beat up the yolks of 3 eggs add to them 1 pt of milk add ¼ oz of Gelatine stir over the fire in a jug till the mixture thickens pour it in spoonfulls in the mould & set to cool. Flavouring & sugar to taste.

1 pint of milk
3 oz of lavender sugar
3 large eggs
2 packets of gelatine OR 2 tablespoons of cornflour
2 x 8 oz packets of sponge fingers or boudoir biscuits
About 10 glacé cherries, halved
One stick of glacé angelica

❧

This is a set custard poured over a biscuit core.

1. *First make the custard:* Put the milk on to warm through.
2. Add the sugar (I used sugar scented with lavender, but sugar stored with a vanilla pod would work just as well, or if you don't mind the extra work warm the milk through with the vanilla pod in it and leave to infuse for about 15 minutes).
3. Separate the eggs, and save the whites for something else.
4. Gently stir the egg yolks into the warmed milk.
5. Dissolve the gelatine in a little boiling water and stir into the custard, mixing thoroughly. Alternatively, mix the cornflour with a little water and use this to thicken the custard.
6. *Now prepare the mould:* While the custard is cooking, line a 2 pint pudding basin with some of the sponge fingers. Break up the remaining fingers and place into the lined bowl.
7. Gently pour in the custard and leave for at least 3 hours to cool.
8. Loosen with a palette knife, turn

**out and decorate with the cherries and angelica**.

*Comments*: Using gelatine to set the custard was tricky, as modern gelatine sets when cooling; whereas the gelatine available to Mary Jane appeared to thicken as it melted into the custard. My personal preference for this recipe is cornflour, which is easier to use, and thickens in the hot custard as Mary Jane intended.

We did not have a Charlotte mould and so made it in a pudding basin, and decorated it afterwards instead of putting the decorations in first as Mary Jane described.

Time – about 30 minutes with 10 minutes for the decoration when serving.

This is a pudding which will act as good base for a variety of flavours as it is a bland mixture of set custard and sponge fingers. A richer flavour will come from making an old English custard set only by egg yolks in which case you will need 6 large eggs instead.

You can put grated lemon rind in with the custard, and a glass of sherry will flavour the sponge biscuits. Other similar recipes suggest using stale cake to fill the centre of the mould too. Treat it as a set trifle and make it anything you want. Can also be served with a fruit coulis.

Very decorative and once over the gelatine hurdle, very simple to make!

Keeping – it didn't last long enough for us to find out.

*Cooked in:* **Aga**
*Tested by:* **Helena Cave-Penney and Simon Best**

*Crystal Palace Pudding*

# Crystal Palace Pudding

> Disolve ½ an ounce of gelatine in one pt of milk allow it to get
> thoroughly hot & not boil pour on 2 well beaten eggs add sugar to taste &
> ½ a wineglassful of sherry & a few drops of Vanella crumbled sponge
> Cake pour into mould & let it stand till set.

1 pint milk
1 sachet gelatine
2 eggs, beaten
2 tablespoons granulated sugar
2 ½ fl oz sherry
5 sponge fingers or 4 trifle sponges,
crumbled fine
½ teaspoon vanilla essence

1. Set aside a 1 pint fancy jelly-mould filled with cold water
2. In a saucepan heat the milk.
3. When hot, sprinkle on the gelatine and stir well to dissolve.
4. Continue stirring until mixture is very hot (but not boiling).
5. Add the eggs and stir very quickly to mix them in before they start to set.
6. Remove pan from heat.
7. Stir in sugar, sherry, sponge cake and vanilla essence.
8. Leave to cool a little, but do not let it start to set.
9. When the mixture is warm rather than hot, empty the water out of the jelly-mould, pour in the mixture and allow to set, finishing off in the fridge.
10. Serve with sponge fingers and whipped cream.

*Comments:* Set in a fancy mould this makes an attractive dessert. It is basically set custard and sponge cake, but the sherry definitely adds interest. Surprisingly, this is quite a filling dessert. This quantity easily serves four.

*Cooked on:* **Conventional electric hob**
*Tested by:* **Katy Jordan**

# Caramel Pudding

Put a good handfull of loaf sugar in a saucepan to boil when it has become a dark brown completely cover the bottom of a mould & let it set make a custard by mixing the yolks & whites of 5 eggs with enough milk to fill the mould sweeten with sugar. Butter the sides of the mould after the sugar is set & strane in the custard put in a steamer & cook.

*Caramel:*
4 oz granulated sugar
2 tbs water

*Custard:*
4 eggs
1 pint milk
1 ½ oz caster sugar

1. Put sugar and water into a pan and dissolve sugar gently.
2. When every grain has melted and not before, boil syrup rapidly without stirring until golden.
3. Take pan off heat and plunge base into cold water for a few seconds to lower the heat and prevent the caramel darkening any further.
4. Use the caramel to coat base and lower sides of a 1½ pint lightly oiled dish.
5. Beat eggs together.
6. Heat milk and sugar in a pan and when almost boiling pour over the eggs stirring briskly.
7. Strain custard into the caramel-lined dish.
8. Cook with bowl sitting in a saucepan half-filled with water. Simmer for one hour until set and knife comes out clean.
9. Turn out when cold so that the caramel coats the top and sides of the custard shape.

*Comments:* As Mary Jane's list of ingredients and method were incomplete we used a recipe which was as near as possible. We first looked up a 2nd edition of Mrs Beeton and the *Parkinson Cookery Book* dating from the late 1930s, but in the end we used a current favourite from Rachel-Mary's own recipe book as this seemed the most similar.

A well-tried and tested recipe. Definitely a cold pudding not a hot one.

*Cooked on:* **Gas hob**

*Tested by:* **Christine Clist and Rachel-Mary Perry**

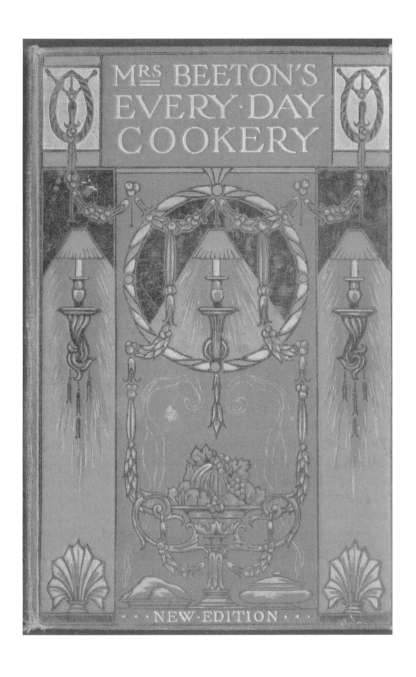

# Chocolate Cream

Melt an 1oz of gelatine in cold water desolve 4 oz plain chocolate grated with as little water as possible & stir over the fire to a stiff paste.  Boil 1 ½ pts of milk with the Gelatine add Chocolate with sugar to taste & essence of Lemon.  Remove from fire add the well beaten yokes of 2 eggs stir well & when getting cold set to cool.

2 sachets of powdered gelatine
1 ½ pints of milk
4 oz good plain cooking chocolate
1-2 tablespoons sugar, or to taste
3 teaspoon lemon essence
Beaten yolks of 2 eggs

1. Melt 2 sachets of powdered gelatine in a cup of boiling milk, then add to the rest of the hot milk.
2. Melt the chocolate in a basin placed over and into a saucepan of boiling water.
3. To the milk and gelatine mixture add the melted chocolate, sugar, and lemon essence.
4. Remove from heat, add the beaten egg yolks and stir well.
5. Pour into a bowl or rinsed mould and chill until set.

*Comments:* We had this for dessert at our 'Mary Jane Stratton' dinner party.  I didn't add sugar, but the tasters were divided on this and some felt sugar would have been a better idea.  My baby daughter loved it.

*Cooked on:* **Gas hob**
*Tested by:* **Kate Robinson**

# Mrs. Gale's Rhubarb Sponge

Cut up 1 ½ lbs of Red Rhubarb in lengths.  Put in a deep pie dish with 1 lb of loaf sugar, ½ pt of water.  Stew in the oven untill well cooked, then dessolve ½ oz of Jelatine in a ¼ pt of Hot Water.  Mix it when cool with the Grated rind of 1 Lemon & the juice of a ½ Lemon, the white of 1 egg & 1 pt of Rhubarb juice.  Whisk this altogether untill it's a stiff froth then add the crumbs of two sponge Biscuits and a few drops of chocineal.  Pour into a mould when set turn out & serve with stiffly whipped Cream in the centre, or it may be served on a Glass dish with whipped cream round.

1½ lb rhubarb, not very red
1 lb sugar
½ pint of water
2 sachets gelatine
Rind of 1 lemon
Juice of half a lemon
White of 1 egg
Two sponge finger biscuits (or more if you prefer)
Red food colouring

1. Stew the rhubarb with the sugar and water until cooked.  Allow to cool a little.

2. Strain the rhubarb through a sieve, and discard the rhubarb pulp.

3. Add two sachets of gelatine to the hot rhubarb juice, making sure they dissolve completely.

4. Mix together the lemon rind and juice, food colouring and rhubarb juice.  Allow to cool.

5. When mixture begins to set, whisk it well until all the mixture a stiff froth.

6. Added the crushed sponge fingers and pour into a wetted mound to set.

7. When fully set, turn out and decorate with whipped cream.

*Mrs Gale's Rhubarb Sponge*

*Comments:* If the mixture isn't cooled and beginning to set when you whisk it, it separates out during the setting stage. This does, however, produce an interesting two-layer effect, and you may prefer this.

It is a very mild tasting rhubarb sponge jelly, which was surprisingly filling. It wasn't as sweet as I expected with the amount of sugar there is in it. Goes well with cream.

I would suggest using less sugar and more sponge biscuits on future occasions. Should keep well as it contains gelatine, but we ate it all before we could find out.

You can use the rhubarb pulp that is left over to make gooseberry and rhubarb turnovers (see p.31).

*Cooked on:* **Rayburn hob**
*Tested by:* **Helena Cave-Penney**

*An hour should be fixed, usually 10 or 9 p.m., after which no servant should be allowed to stay out. To permit breaches of this rule, without having good and explicit reasons furnished, is very far from being a kindness to the servant concerned. The moral responsibility for evil that may result rests largely on the employer who permits late hours.*

*Especial care is needed with young girls. They should be given opportunities for welcoming respectable friends at their employer's house, and not be forced by absence of such provision for their comfort to spend their spare time out of doors, often in driving rain, possibly in bad company.* (Mrs. Beeton)

# Raspberry Sponge

Soak 1 oz Jelatine in ½ pt cold water for ¼ hour then add 1 pt boiling water when cool add ½ lb sugar & ½ pint of Raspberry juice or jam the juice of 1 Lemon & whites of 2 eggs. Whisk it for ½ an hour, pour into the shape serve with cream sauce or Custard.

½ oz gelatine (1 sachet)
15 fl. oz hot water
6 oz frozen raspberries, defrosted
4 oz caster sugar
juice of ½ lemon
White of 1 large egg

1. Put the water in a large mixing bowl and sprinkle the gelatine into it and stir. Leave for about 15 minutes or until dissolved.
2. Rub the raspberries through a sieve until only the pips are left. This should yield about ¼ pint of raspberry pulp.
3. Add the sugar, lemon juice, raspberry pulp and egg white to the mixture and whisk with an electric whisk for 5-10 minutes. Pour into a glass bowl (big enough to hold three pints), and leave to set in the fridge for 3-4 hours.
4. The result is a thin layer of raspberry jelly at the bottom, with a thick layer of dark pink froth above.
5. Serves 4-6.

*Comments:* The flavour is good, and the leftovers were fine a day later (my daughter Eleanor ate most of them – she thought it was great as an after-school snack) so it could easily be made the day before it's needed. We didn't bother with cream or custard, as it didn't seem to lack anything. It looks very pretty in a glass bowl.

*Tested by:* **Helen Williams**

# Lemon Cream

2 Lemons    🌿   1 pt Water   🌿   2 oz Cornflower   🌿   6 oz Sugar
🌿   2 eggs

Peel the Lemons thinely & boil the rind with the water 5 minutes.  Mix
the cornflower smoothly with the strained juice of the Lemons.  Add the
licquid from the rinds & boil 3 minutes, stiring all the time, add sugar &
cool slightly, mix in the well beaten eggs & stir over gentle fire till they
thicken, pour into a wet mould, when cold turn out.

2 lemons
1 pt water
2 oz cornflour
6 oz sugar
2 large eggs

∽◦∽

1. Zest the lemons, or peel the zest very thinly off the white pith.
2. Put zest in saucepan with water and bring to the boil.  Boil for five minutes.
3. Squeeze the lemons.
4. In a basin beat the eggs well and set aside.
5. In a saucepan mix the cornflour smoothly with the lemon juice, a little at a time.  It will be quite thick.
6. Strain the water to remove the lemon zest.
7. Gradually add the water to the cornflour mix.  At this stage the mixture will be quite thin.
8. Bring to the boil, and boil gently for three minutes, stirring all the time.  The mixture will thicken.
9. Remove from heat and stir in the sugar.
10. Cool very slightly for a minute or two.
11. Add the beaten eggs.  They need beating in quite assertively.
12. Put the mixture back onto a gentle heat and stir continuously until the mixture thickens like custard.  This takes 5-10 minutes.
13. Rinse a jelly mould with cold

water, then pour in the mixture and leave to set.

would look very pretty set in a fancy jelly-mould.

*Comments:* This has a really strong lemon flavour. It sets very well and

*Cooked on:* **Conventional electric hob**

*Tested by:* **Katy Jordan**

# Lemon or Orange Solid

Soak 1 oz Sheet Jelatine in enough Cold Water to cover it. Rub the rind of 3 lemons or oranges on 1 lb of Loaf Sugar. First boil the sugar & Gelatine & Rinds cut very thin in 1 pt of milk only just let it boil then pour on to the mixture 1 pt of cold milk. Let it stand till nearly cold & then add the juice of 3 Lemons or 6 Oranges, put in mould when cold turn out.

1 pt milk
1 oz gelatine (2 sachets)
3 oranges
2 oz cube sugar (or to taste)

1. Sprinkle the gelatine into ¼ pint of milk.
2. Rub the sugar cubes on the orange rind to absorb some of the oil.
3. Peel the oranges very thinly and chop the rind into slivers.
4. Put the sugar, orange rind and gelatine into a saucepan, together with another ¼ pint of milk.
5. Bring to the boil, remove from the heat and add the remaining ½ pint cold milk. Allow to cool.
6. When nearly cold, add the juice of the 3 oranges, stir and pour in-to the mould. Put into the fridge to set.

7. Once it has set turn it out onto a plate. There will be a pale orange milk jelly on top and with a brighter orange layer below.

*Comments:* ½ oz gelatine is not enough for 1 pint milk: the juice of the oranges is nearly another ½ pint and it does need the extra gelatine. This was a lot of effort, especially fiddling with the orange rinds. The girls liked the milk jelly but not the orange layer. We thought it was good overall, though I thought it a bit sweet so I have greatly reduced the sugar to compensate. If you want to make the lemon version, half the amount of fruit juice will give a good strong lemony flavour.

*Cooked on:* **Aga hob**
*Tested by:* **Helen Williams**

# Apple Jelly

1 lb of apples ❦ ½ pt of Water ❦ 1 Lemon rind & juice ❦ 3 oz Sugar Castor ❦ ½ oz sheet Gelatine

Peel & slice the apples put in a saucepan with thinely cut Lemon rind sugar water & Lemon juice. Simmer till tender put through a hair Sieve melt the Gelatine in ½ a gill of water & strain it, set in a mould. Gooseberries & Rhubarb done the same way. Allow ¾ oz gelatine & more sugar.

1 lb cooking apples
½ pint water
3 oz caster sugar
1 lemon
1 sachet of gelatine

᪥

1. Peel and slice apples.
2. Put into a saucepan with thinly pared lemon rind, juice and sugar.
3. Simmer until apples are soft and the liquid well reduced.
4. Strain through a fine sieve or jelly cloth.
5. Melt the gelatine and add to the apple liquid as the sachet directions instruct.
6. Pour into a jelly mould or shape that has been rinsed with cold water.
7. Allow to set.

*Comments:* I sieved the apples twice and left a few pieces of lemon in to make it look more interesting. You could add some blackberries to give it more colour. It has a pleasant taste, well-balanced, though I do think the jelly was a little stiff – but that does depend on ones personal taste.

*Cooked on:* **Gas hob**
*Tested by:* **Sheila Page**

# Egg Jelly

¾ oz of Jelatine 🌿 1 pt Water 🌿 4 oz sugar 🌿 The Grated rind & strained juice of 1 Lemon 🌿 Well beaten yolks of 4 eggs

Soak the Jelatine in the water for about 10 minutes then place in a stew pan with the sugar 1 Lemon & stir over the fire until the mixture comes to the simering point. Have ready the well beaten yolks of the eggs in a baisen add to the other contents in the stew pan stir over the fire a few minutes but do not let it boil. When nearly cold strain into a mould.

4 large eggs
1 lemon
1 pint very hot water
1 sachet powdered gelatine
4 oz granulated sugar

1. Fill a 1 pint jelly-mould with cold water and set aside.
2. Separate the eggs and beat the yolks in a basin.
3. Grate the zest of the lemon into another basin. Squeeze the lemon and add juice to zest.
4. Pour 1 pint of almost boiling water into a measuring jug, and sprinkle on the gelatine, stirring to dissolve.
5. In a saucepan put the sugar, lemon juice and zest, pour on the gelatine mixture, and heat gently until it is almost simmering.
6. Add the egg yolks and stir quickly to incorporate them completely into the jelly.
7. Continue stirring over a gentle heat for a few minutes. Do not let it boil.
8. Set aside to cool until it is luke-warm.
9. Empty cold water out of jelly-mould and pour in the cooled jelly. Place in the fridge to set.
10. Just before serving turn jelly out onto a fancy plate.

*Comments:* I had an anxious moment while I was adding the egg yolks to the hot jelly. For a moment I thought that the egg was going to cook in streamers within the jelly like a jelly ripple. Frantic stirring prevented this happening.

    This makes a lemony set dessert, which is a cross between jelly and solid egg custard. It doesn't sound very appetising put like that, but I enjoyed it very much. Set in a fancy mould it looks very pretty.

*Cooked on:* **Electric hob**
*Tested by:* **Katy Jordan**

# Apricot Eggs

Make a good cornflower Blancmange pour into wet saucers when set turn
out arrange on a Flat dish on each place half a tinned apricot & scatter
finely chopped Pistachie nuts on each to look like chopped parsly on
poached eggs.

*Blancmange*  ⚜  Take 2 ½ oz or 5 tablespoonfull of Cornflower  ⚜
2 pts or 3 large breakfast cups of milk
Boil 10 minutes.  Flavouring to taste.  B.M. with egg, add 2 yolks of eggs
before boiling for 10 minutes.

1 pint milk
1¼ oz cornflour
1-2 tablespoons sugar, or to taste.
Vanilla essence
4 tinned apricot halves
Pistachio nuts (not roasted or
salted!)

1. Mix the cornflour with a little of
the milk.
2. Add the sugar to sweeten as you
prefer, and stir well.
3. Bring the rest of the milk to the
boil.
4. Remove from the heat and add
the cornflour mixture to it.
Return to heat and boil for 10
minutes.
5. Pour into four saucers which

have been rinsed in cold water
and leave to set.
6. When set, turn out onto a flat
plate, and put an apricot half on
each and sprinkle with chopped
pistachio nuts.

*Comments:*   Mary Jane doesn't
specifically include sugar in her
blancmange recipe, but having (dis-
astrously) made these without, I am
convinced that this is a mistake: do
not forget the sugar.  Apricots go
nicely with vanilla, so I've suggested
you add that as flavouring.

This was a really silly dessert,
fun for children and good as a joke
for adults!

*Cooked on:* **Aga hob**
*Tested by:* **Helen Williams**

# 5

# Cakes Large & Small

❧

**B**utter is of the first importance in cake-making, and where a rich cake is desired of fine flavour and keeping qualities, only the best butter should be used. But in most instances it will be desirable to use a somewhat cheaper fat for the purposes of cake-making, especially where the family is large and the means limited . . . Of late years so many improvements have been introduced into the manufacture of margarine and other butter substitutes that almost an expert is required to tell the difference . . .

After butter the eggs next claim attention . . . For making cakes, eggs that are from 7 to 14 days old, provided they are properly kept, are best . . .

Refined sugars can now be procured at so low a price, already ground and pulverised, that it is more economical to buy it in this form that to use loaf sugar and pound it . . .

With the introduction of machinery for fruit cleaning purposes, currants can be procured comparatively clean... in almost every case washing is not at all necessary... Sultanas, although they are no doubt cleaned, require carefully picking over and a good rub on a coarse sieve will remove almost the whole of the sprigs, which are a very objectionable ingredient in a cake. Raisins should in all cases be stoned, and if a large quantity has to be prepared, a small machine suitable for the purpose can be procured from the household stores or ironmongers for a few shillings.

Flour for cakes should always be of the finest quality procurable, and for best goods Vienna is the most suitable for use, and will also give the best results. But for all ordinary purposes of the household, what is termed "Whites" is suitable. But in any case let the flour be dry to the touch and sweet to the smell, with some colour and strength.

*Mrs Beeton (1907), pp.1406-8.*

Mary Jane had collected many different cake recipes, from simple sponges to solid fruitcakes, and I have included a representative selection here. Nowadays, cakes are available from every supermarket and local shop, so that there is apparently little incentive to spend time on baking them ourselves. But my testers showed great enthusiasm for the cake recipes, and it is clear that there is a fair amount of home baking still going on. And why not? Home-made cakes are wonderful, and don't actually take a great deal of time to make, if you have the right tins to hand, and a good electric mixer. So go ahead, and rediscover the satisfaction of making a fine cake for Sunday tea.

*It is a thousand times tested truth that without early rising and punctuality good work is almost impossible. A cook ought to realize this important fact, for if she lose an hour in the morning, she is likely to be kept toiling all day to overtake necessary tasks that would otherwise have been easy to her. Six o'clock is a good hour to rise in the summer, and seven in the winter.* (Mrs. Beeton)

# Jam Sandwich

2 eggs ❦ their weight of Butter Sugar & Flour

Melt the butter in a baisen to cream it add sugar flour & eggs beat all
for a quarter of an hour put the mixture in a shallow tin & bake in a
quick oven cut in half spread jam between cut in Sandwiches.

4 oz butter
4 oz caster sugar
4 oz Self-Raising flour
½ teaspoon baking powder
2 eggs = 4 oz weight

❧

1. Preheat oven to 180°C / 350°F / Gas 4.
2. Leave butter in warm place until very soft but not oily.
3. Add sugar, sifted flour, baking powder and eggs.
4. Beat in a food mixer for 2 minutes until light in colour and creamy.
5. Spoon into a greased 8-inch loose-bottomed sandwich tin.
6. Cook for 20 minutes until springy to touch. If using Aga, cook in main oven with plain shelf above.
7. When cool, split sponge and fill with jam.

*Comments:* For my first attempt at this recipe I followed the original ingredients closely, but found it produced a heavy-textured, brittle, rather biscuity cake. So I added half a teaspoon of baking powder to the ingredients, and this was much more successful, light and spongy. You could use soft margarine instead of butter to make the sponge even lighter.

A good all-in-one sponge recipe.

*Cooked in:* **Aga**
*Tested by:* **Sue Chadwick**

# Phyllis's Sponge Cake

4 eggs   🌺   Their weight in Castor Sugar   🌺   The weight of 2 eggs in
Self Raising Flour.

Beat for 20 minutes eggs & Castor Sugar, then sprinkle in Flour & beat
lightly.  Butter large tin with 1 oz Flour & 1 teaspoonfull of butter
warmed on stove.  Pin on the outside of tin Buttered Paper, the paper to
be 2 inches above tin.  Bake in a moderate oven 1 ½ hours.

4 eggs
9 oz caster sugar (= weight of 4
eggs)
5 oz Self-Raising flour (= weight of
2 eggs)

*ᘓᘍᘖ*

1. Preheat oven to 180°C/ 350°F /
   Gas 4.
2. Grease and flour a 9-inch loose-
   bottomed sponge tin.
3. With an electric beater, whisk the
   eggs and sugar together until the
   mixture is light and fluffy, and

increased in bulk.
4. Gradually fold in the sifted flour.
5. Pour mixture into the prepared
   tin, and bake for 30-35 minutes.
6. Turn out of tin, and when cool,
   split and sandwich together with
   jam.

*Comments:* This is basically a fatless
sponge.  It rose well and held its
shape.  As with all fatless sponges,
this tends to be dry.

*Cooked in:* **Electric fan oven**
*Tested by:* **Sue Chadwick**

# Swiss Roll

2 eggs  ✥  3 oz Sifted Sugar  ✥  2 oz Sifted Flour  ✥  2 table
spoonfull of milk  ✥  ½ tea spoonfull of Baking Powder  ✥  Jam

Whist eggs & sugar for 20 minutes mix in flour lightly do not stir or beat add
milk sprinkle baking Powder when baked lay on Sugared Paper & Roll.

2 eggs
2 oz caster sugar
2 oz Self-Raising flour
jam

෴

1. Preset oven to 200°C / 400°F / Gas 6.
2. Line a swiss roll tin (7 x 11-inch) with baking parchment.
3. Whisk eggs and sugar together until pale, thick and creamy.
4. LIGHTLY fold in sifted flour.
5. Pour into swiss roll tin and bake for about 12 minutes until golden and springy to the touch.
6. Turn out onto damp tea towel sprinkled with caster sugar, and peel off paper.
7. Quickly spread with warm jam, make a score 1 inch up on each long side and using tea towel roll

up away from you. Leave for about 30 secs covered with cloth. This method will stop the roll cracking.

*Comments:* I approached this with some dread after Katy's bad experience but actually it went exceedingly well. I decided the list of ingredients should be changed a little aiming at a better result. Took out an ounce of the sugar to make it less sweet. I thought milk would make the sponge heavy and it seemed unnecessary. I also decided to go with Self-Raising flour rather than plain and baking powder, because the secret of this sort of mix, I always think, is in the lightness of the flour, hence I made sure the flour was well sifted.

I was surprised it behaved so well. I did not bother with whisking

over hot water but followed the instructions as set, so this ended up
being a really easy and successful
recipe.

*Cooked in:* **Conventional electric oven**
*Tested by:* **Sue Chadwick, after Katy made**
**a complete inedible mess of it – twice!**

*Neatness should be studied by all engaged in domestic work...*
*Clear as you go; do not allow a host of basins, spoons, plates, etc. to*
*accumulate on the dresser or tables while you are preparing the dinner.*
*It is as easy to put a thing in its place when it is done with as to*
*continually remove it to find room for fresh requisites.* (Mrs. Beeton)

*Economy. - Never waste or throw away anything that can be*
*turned to account... Go early every morning to your larder (which, like*
*the kitchen, ought to be kept perfectly clean and neat), and while*
*changing plates, looking to your bread pan (which should always be*
*emptied and wiped out every morning), take notice if there is anything*
*not likely to keep...* (Mrs. Beeton)

*Do not let your stock of pepper, salt, spices, seasoning, herbs,*
*etc., dwindle so low that there is danger of finding yourself minus some*
*very important ingredient, the lack of which may cause much confusion*
*and annoyance.* (Mrs. Beeton)

# Mocha Cake

4 eggs ❦ 4 oz Castor Sugar ❦ 4 oz Flour dry & sifted ❦ 1 oz of Cornflower ❦ 1 teaspoonfull of Lemon juice.

Beat up the whites of the eggs stiffly and add a little to the yolks & then add a little of the mixed & sifted flour & so alternately untill a smooth paste is formed. Line a round cake tin with buttered paper, place the mixture in it & bake in a moderate oven for ¾ of an hour. When baked & cold cut it into three layers & place a thick layer of coffee butter between each layer of cake. Press it together & ice it with coffee iceing.

4 oz Self-Raising flour
1 oz cornflour
4 oz caster sugar
4 large eggs
1 teaspoonful lemon juice

1. Pre-heat oven to 180°C / 350°F / Gas°4.
2. Line a 7-inch round cake tin.
3. Sift flour with cornflour and caster sugar.
4. Separate yolks of eggs from whites.
5. Beat whites of eggs until they stand in stiff peaks.
6. Break up yolks of eggs in a large mixing bowl.
7. Add lemon juice and beat briefly.
8. Using a metal spoon, fold in beaten whites and flour mixture alternately.
9. Turn into the cake tin, smooth top and make a well in the centre to allow for cake rising.
10. Bake in centre of oven for 45 minutes.
11. When cold, cut into three layers and sandwich together with thick layers of coffee butter (see p.75).
12. Ice with coffee icing (see p.75) and decorate with cherries or sugar strands.

*Comments:* This is a fatless sponge, so has the texture of a gateau. The

butter cream and icing add moist-
ness.

Another very popular cake
that got eaten very quickly by willing
testers. Not an everyday cake, but
good for a special tea when you want

to impress someone with your
culinary skills.

*Cooked in:*  **Conventional electric oven**
*Tested by:*  **Katy Jordan**

# Coffee Butter & Icing

*For Coffee Butter*
4 oz of Iceing sugar & a little coffee esence ❀ 4 oz of butter

Beat it to a stiff Butter.

*For Coffee Iceing*
¾ lb of Iceing Sugar ❀ Beaten whites of 2 eggs ❀ 1 Teaspoonful of Lemon juice ❀ Coffee esence to Flavour ❀ enough water to mix to a smooth paste

Stand the cake on a saucer in a dish & pour the Iceing over it when it is set decorate with some of the coffee Butter using a bag to pipe & decorate with cherries etc Pistacie nuts.

*Coffee Butter*
4 oz icing sugar
1 teasp. coffee essence
4 oz butter

*Coffee Icing*
Beaten white of 1 large egg
½ teaspoon lemon juice
6 oz icing sugar
1 teaspoon coffee essence
Water

❧

1. Make the coffee butter by beating all the ingredients together until well creamed.
2. Sandwich the cake together as directed in the Mocha Cake recipe (see p.73).
3. Make the coffee icing by first beating the egg-white until it stands in peaks.
4. Add the lemon juice and coffee essence and beat again.
5. Gradually add the sifted icing sugar, beating between additions.
6. Invert a tea-plate on a dinner plate and stand the cake on the tea-plate.
7. Use a wide-bladed knife dipped in hot water to spread the icing

sugar all over the cake until the top and sides are coated.

8. Decorate with piped coffee butter, cherries, or coffee-coloured sugar strands.

9. Any drips of icing will fall onto the dinner plate, and once the icing is set you can move the cake to a clean serving plate.

*Comments:* Mary Jane's original butter cream quantities were just right, but I found the coffee icing amount was very generous so I have halved the amounts.

You can vary the amount of coffee essence you use to make the flavour more or less strong.

*Tested by:* **Katy Jordan**

*Make a rule to send everything up to table really well cooked. Do not regard this as an impossibility for it can be done.* (Mrs. Beeton)

*A dirty kitchen is a disgrace to all concerned. Good cookery cannot exist without absolute cleanliness. It takes no longer to keep a kitchen clean and orderly than untidy and dirty, for the time that is spent in keeping it in good order is saved when culinary operations are going on and everything is clean and in its place. Personal cleanliness is most necessary, particularly with regard to the hands.* (Mrs. Beeton)

*When at your work, dress suitably; wear short dresses, well-fitting boots, and large aprons with bibs, or which every cook and kitchen-maid should have a good supply, and you will be comfortable as you never can be with long dresses, small aprons, and slipshod shoes.* (Mrs. Beeton)

# Madeira Cake

3 eggs ❦ rind of 1 Lemon ❦ 6 oz lump sugar ❦ ½ gill of water

Make a syrup of these & add the eggs to it at boiling point beat it keeping all as hot as possible for 15 minutes then add 5 oz Flour warmed & 2 oz Butter creamed beat well pour into a mould bake 15 minutes then add a slice of citron on top & bake 15 more minutes.

6 oz caster sugar
3 fl. oz water
Rind of 1 lemon, cut very thin and chopped small
3 eggs, beaten
5 oz plain flour (warmed)
2 oz butter/margarine, softened

1. Preset oven to 180°C / 350°F / Gas 4.
2. Put sugar, water and lemon rind in a pan.
3. Heat gently until the sugar has dissolved, then bring to the boil. Remove from the heat and add the eggs, beating the mixture for 5 minutes with an electric whisk.
4. Beat in the flour and margarine.
5. Put in a greased cake tin: the mixture is very runny so it is best to avoid loose-bottomed tins.
6. Bake in a moderate oven for 1-1¼ hours.
7. Add a slice of preserved citron peel half way through cooking if desired.

*Comments:* My first two attempts were not good: in spite of looking fine, they were uncooked in the middle. I deduced that the cooking time is wrong. Third time lucky: I followed a mixture of Mrs. Beeton and standard Madeira cake recipes for the cooking times and it worked.

The cake has a solid moist texture and pleasantly lemony flavour.

*Cooked in:* **Aga**
*Tested by:* **Helen Williams**

# Orange Cake

3 eggs ❦ Equal weights in Butter sugar & Flour ❦ 2 oranges juice
❦ Baking Powder

6 oz butter
6 oz caster sugar
3 large eggs
6 oz Self-Raising flour
Grated rind and juice of 1 orange
A few drops of orange essence
6 oz icing sugar

❧

1. Grease and line an 8-inch square cake tin.
2. Preset the oven to 170°C / 325°F / Gas 3.
3. Cream the butter until light and fluffy.
4. Add the sugar and cream both together.
5. Beat the eggs lightly in a separate bowl, add orange essence, then beat into creamed mixture a very little at a time.
6. Sir in grated orange rind.
7. Fold in flour.
8. Turn out into tin, and bake in top half of oven for 30-35 minutes, until golden brown, springy to the touch, and shrinking away from the sides of the tin.
9. Set aside for 10 minutes, then turn out of tin and cool.
10. *Make the glacé icing:* mix icing sugar with one tablespoonful of orange juice, then if necessary add tiny amounts of juice to bring the mixture to the point where it will coat the back of a wooden spoon.
11. Spread glacé icing over cake and smooth with broad-bladed knife dipped in hot water. Decorate with orange and lemon jelly slices.

*Comments:* On my first attempt I added the juice of two oranges to the mixture, and ended up with an overly moist sponge cake which didn't really taste of oranges. So I used orange rind and essence to flavour the sponge, and used some orange juice to make a flavoured icing.

The mixture has the same proportions of ingredients as a classic Victoria sponge, so if you prefer you can bake it in two 7-inch sponge tins, and sandwich the sponges together with buttercream flavoured with orange juice.

This makes a well-balanced cake, with the sweetness of the icing balanced by the plain (but very good) sponge.

*Cooked in:* **Conventional electric oven**
*Tested by:* **Katy Jordan**

*A lady should never allow herself to forget the important duty of watching over the moral and physical welfare of those beneath her roof. Without seeming unduly inquisitive, she can always learn something of their acquaintances and holiday occupation, and should, when necessary, warn them against the dangers and evils of bad company.*
(Mrs. Beeton)

# Manchester Cake

4 oz Butter   6 oz Flour   6 oz sugar   4 oz Cocoanut   1 gill of milk   2 eggs

4 oz butter
6 oz caster sugar
2 large eggs
6 oz Self-Raising flour
4 oz sweetened dessicated coconut
5 fl. oz pint of milk
6 oz icing sugar
1-2 tablespoons water
Dessicated coconut for decoration
Glacé cherries

1. Grease and line an 8-inch square cake tin.
2. Preset oven to 170°C / 325°F / Gas 3.
3. Beat butter until it is light and fluffy.
4. Add sugar to butter and cream them together.
5. Beat eggs separately in a basin, then beat into creamed mixture a very little at a time.
6. Fold in flour with metal spoon.
7. Stir in the coconut.
8. Stir in the milk.
9. Turn out into the tin, and bake in top of oven for 35-40 minutes.
10. Set aside to cool for 10 minutes, then turn out of tin and leave to get cold.
11. Make glacé icing by adding water a very little at a time to the icing sugar, so that it doesn't get too runny. It is the right consistency when it coats the back of a spoon.
12. Spread icing over the cake with a broad-bladed knife dipped in hot water.
13. Sprinkle with dessicated coconut and decorate with glace cherries if you feel it needs some colour.

*Comments:* Mary Jane doesn't suggest icing the cake, but I found that, as with the Orange cake, the icing just makes the cake that bit more special. The coconut flavour comes over very well without being overwhelming.

 Why 'Manchester' cake? Probably because of the ships that

arrived at the port carrying goods from the West Indies, including coconuts.

*Cooked in:* **Conventional electric oven**

*Tested by:* **Katy Jordan**

*Cooking by gas has been much on the increase in late years, the gas companies in various localities lending all the aid in their power to further it by supplying their customers with gas stoves, or ranges, at a low annual rental. Cooking by gas has much to recommend it. Gas kitcheners are compact, as no space has to be provided for furnace or ash-pit... And they are easily managed even by inexperienced girls.*
(Mrs. Beeton)

*A well-constructed, cleanly kept and well-managed oil stove will cook food as well as any other stove or corresponding capacity; and with proper care there should be neither smoke nor odour from the flame... In a properly constructed stove there is not much danger from explosion, unless a light is, through carelessness, brought in contact with the oil.* (Mrs. Beeton)

*Cooking by electricity is now quite practicable, though for the present decidedly expensive. There is practically no loss of heat, as the electrical connexion is only made when cooking is in actual progress. The system also of course ensures freedom from dust and dirt... As some municipalities are now supplying the electric current in the daytime at as low a rate as 2d. per Board of Trade unit, it is probably that cooking by electricity is destined to undergo a rapid development.*
(Mrs. Beeton)

# Ginger Bread Cake

1 lb of Treacle   🌿   ¼ lb of Butter   🌿   ¼ lb Sugar   🌿   1 ½ lbs of Flour
🌿   ½ oz Ginger   🌿   ½ oz Allspice   🌿   1 teaspoonfull of Baking Powder
🌿   ¼ teaspoonful of Carbonate Soda   🌿   ¼ pt of Milk   🌿   1 egg

Put the Butter into the Flour.  Mix all the other ingredients in by degrees.
Bake in a Slow oven about 1 hour.  It usually takes much longer.

2 oz butter
12 oz plain flour
¼ oz ground ginger
¼ oz allspice
½ teaspoonful baking powder
⅛ teaspoonful bicarbonate of soda
1 small egg
5 fluid oz milk
8 oz black treacle
2 oz caster sugar

∽◌∾

1. Grease and line a 12 x 7-inch cake tin.
2. Preset the oven to 170°C / 325°F / Gas 3.
3. Rub butter into flour.
4. Add spices, bicarbonate of soda and baking powder.
5. Melt together treacle and sugar but don't allow to boil.
6. Beat egg and milk together.
7. Add treacle and sugar, egg and milk to dry ingredients.
8. Mix well. The mixture will be quite stiff and putty-like.
9. Turn out into greased tin.
10. Bake for 40 minutes.

*Comments:* This has a good flavour but is rather dry.  It is a heavier cake/slice, not for polite afternoon tea. 'Bread cake' does describe it well. The men suggested it would be good with cream.  It appears to have good keeping potential.

We also tried it with golden syrup, which made a lighter cake, but it did not have such a good flavour.

*Cooked in:* **Conventional electric oven**
*Tested by:* **Christine Clist and Rachel-Mary Perry**

# Scarborough Cake

½ lb of Butter 🌱 6 oz Flour 🌱 6 oz Sifted Sugar 🌱 2 oz Currents
or Sultanas 🌱 3 eggs 🌱 ¼ tea spoonful of Baking Powder 🌱
Candid Peel & Almonds

Bake in a flat tin 3 inches deep for 25 minutes. Strew Almonds on top.
This cake should be cut in fingers & piled on plate.

8 oz butter
6 oz caster sugar
3 large eggs
6 oz plain flour
¼ teaspoon baking powder
2 oz currants
1 oz candied peel
Flaked almonds

1. Line an 8-inch square cake tin, 3 inches deep, with baking parchment.
2. Preheat oven to 190°C / 375°F / Gas 5.
3. Beat butter really well.
4. Add sifted sugar and cream together until mixture is pale and fluffy.
5. Break eggs into a basin and beat them a little to break them up.
6. Gradually beat in the eggs to the creamed mixture, adding a dessertspoon of flour if the mixture curdles.
7. Fold in the sifted flour and baking powder with a metal spoon.
8. Stir in currants and peel.
9. Turn out mixture into lined tin, level the top, and sprinkle generously with flaked almonds.
10. Bake on middle shelf of oven for 25-30 minutes.
11. Serve cut into fingers.

*Comments:* Make sure you beat the mixture really well in the early stages to get as much air as possible into the mixture. This makes a very rich buttery sponge. It keeps well in an airtight container for up to a week. All tasters enjoyed it very much, and one claimed that two slices cured her hangover!

*Cooked in:* **Conventional electric oven**
*Tested by:* **Katy Jordan**

# Phyllis's Lemon Cake

> 1 lb Flour  ❧  ½ Butter  ❧  12 oz Sultanas  ❧  10 oz Sugar  ❧  4 eggs  ❧  Juice & Rind of a Lemon
>
> Beat Butter & Sugar to a Cream add Beaten eggs & then add Lemon juice & Rind & gradually Sultanas & Flour.

8 oz plain flour
4 oz butter
6 oz sultanas
5 oz caster sugar
2 large eggs
Juice and grated rind of half large lemon

❧

1. Line a small loaf tin with baking parchment or greaseproof paper.
2. Preset the oven to 190°C / 375°F / Gas 5.
3. Using a mixer beat the butter until pale and fluffy.
4. Add sugar and beat again to cream butter & sugar together.
5. Beat the eggs well in a bowl and then beat into the mixture, a little at a time.  If the mixture curdles add a little flour.
6. Beat in lemon juice and grated rind.
7. Gradually fold in the sifted flour.
8. Stir in the sultanas.
9. Spoon the mixture into the tin and level the top.
10. Bake in the centre of the oven for 55–60 minutes.

*Comments:*  I thought the original quantities would make rather too large a cake so I halved the ingredients.  There is no raising agent in the cake, so I beat the butter, sugar and eggs really well to get air into the mixture.  This makes a close-textured cake with a very pleasant lemony flavour.  It keeps very well and seems to improve with keeping.

*Cooked in:*  **Conventional electric oven**
*Tested by:*  **Katy Jordan**

# Military Tartlets

Make some Jam Sandwich. Cut into round shapes with fancy cutter take out centre fill with Jam & put a spoonful of cream on top with cherries.

*Genoese Pastry*
4 eggs
6 oz sugar
3 oz butter
6 oz plain flour
½ teaspoon baking powder

*Filling*
Jam
Whipped cream
Cherries (or other fruit to taste)

1. Grease and line two shallow 12-inch by 7-inch cake tins.
2. Preset oven to 180°C / 350°F / Gas 4.
3. Break eggs into a bowl with the sugar.
4. Place this on a saucepan of hot water and beat well for 15 minutes until thick enough to leave a trail.
5. Remove bowl from pan and beat for 5 minutes or until cool.

6. Sift in almost all the flour and stir in carefully.
7. Slightly melt the butter and stir this in.
8. Add baking powder mixed with remaining flour and stir well.
9. Turn mixture into two prepared tins.
10. Bake for 30-40 minutes.
11. Allow to cool and sandwich together with cherry jam.
12. Cut out rounds with a fancy cutter.
13. Remove centre of top sandwich, fill with jam and decorate with a spoonful of cream and cherries.

*Comments:* We searched through recipe books, from 2nd edition Mrs. Beeton to Delia Smith, to find out what 'jam sandwich' might be in this case, and concluded that it should be Genoese pastry. Very nice too!

The scraps left over from making fancy shapes do make excellent trifle.

Pastry appears to keep well
but the cream . . . !

*Cooked in:* **Conventional electric oven**
*Tested by:* **Christine Clist and Rachel-**
**Mary Perry**

## HOW TO MAKE PASTRY.

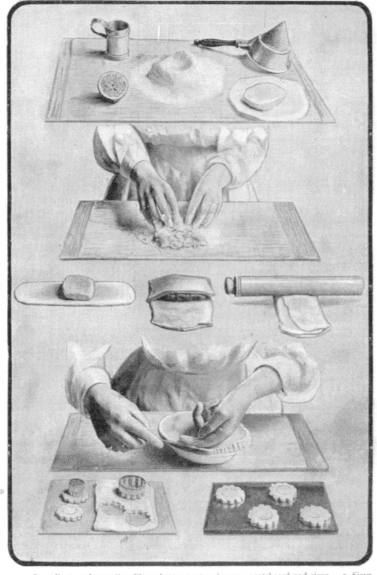

1. Ingredients and utensils : Flour, butter, water, lemon ; pasteboard and sieve.  2. Sieve the flour, add water, and mix with the fingers.  3. Roll out and place the butter in the centre. 4. Fold the ends over, making an envelope for the butter.  5. Roll out.  6. Method of flaking edge of pies.  7. Method of cutting out tartlets or bouches.  8. Tartlets or bouches for baking.

# Phyllis's Queen Cakes

¼ lb Butter  ❧  3 oz Castor Sugar  ❧  6 oz Flour  ❧  4 oz Sultanas
❧  1 tea spoonfull of Baking Powder  ❧  Grated rind of a Lemon  ❧  2
eggs  ❧  A little milk if necessary.

Beat Butter & Sugar to a cream, add other ingredients & mix well.  Bake for
15 minutes in Patty-Pans.

4 oz butter
3 oz caster sugar
2 large eggs
5 oz plain flour
1 teaspoon baking powder
Grated rind of 1 lemon
4 oz sultanas
Milk to mix

1. Preheat the oven to 190°C / 375°F / Gas 4.
2. Oil a bun tin, or use paper cases if you prefer.
3. Beat the butter to a cream.
4. Add the sugar, and beat again to a cream.
5. Beat in the eggs.
6. Fold in the flour and baking powder.

7. Sir in the lemon rind and sultanas.
8. If the mixture is a little stiff, stir in enough milk to mix to a soft dropping consistency.
9. Spoon the mixture into the hollows in the bun tin.
10. Bake on the top shelf for 15-17 minutes.

*Comments:*  This makes 12 cakes. They seemed just as light and spongy as if I had used Self-Raising flour, and were very nice little cakes. To vary the flavour, leave out the rind and fruit, and replace the sugar with 3 tablespoons of honey.

*Cooked in:*  **Conventional electric oven**
*Tested by:*  **Katy Jordan**

# Chocolate Cakes

3 oz Flour ✤ 3 oz Castor Sugar ✤ 2 sticks Chocolate Grated ✤ ½ teaspoonful of Baking Powder ✤ 2 eggs ✤ 2 oz Butter

Beat Butter to a cream add sugar then flour & chocolate mixed together & baking Powder, beat eggs well & add to the dry ingredients.  Bake in patty pans in a quick oven about 10 minutes.

2 oz butter
3 oz caster sugar
3 oz plain flour
2 oz ordinary plain chocolate, grated
½ teaspoon baking powder
2 eggs

❧

1. Preheat oven to 180°C / 350° F / Gas 4.
2. Beat butter until creamy.
3. Beat in sugar until pale and creamy.
4. Add sifted flour and baking powder and grated chocolate.
5. Add well-beaten eggs and mix gently until smooth.
6. Put spoonfuls of mixture into paper bun cases.
7. Cook for 15 minutes.  If using Aga, cook with plain shelf above.
8. Makes 9 buns.

*Comments:* Using chocolate instead of cocoa powder gives these cakes a very nice chocolatey taste.  The texture is substantial – more like American muffins – probably because of using plain flour and baking powder rather than Self-Raising flour.

*Cooked in:* **Aga**
*Tested by:* **Sue Chadwick**

# Chocolate Icing

Grate 2 oz best chocolate put in a saucepan with ½ a gill of hot water & stir
till quite desolved then add ½ a pound of Iceing Sugar & stir again till
quite smooth.

2 oz ordinary plain chocolate
3 tablespoons hot water
8 oz icing sugar sifted

ᗧ~ᗣ

1. Grate chocolate and put in saucepan with 3 tablespoons hot water.
2. Stir until chocolate has melted.
3. Add sifted icing sugar and beat until smooth.

4. Makes enough to ice 36 buns

*Comments:* It could be made more chocolatey by reducing the water to 2 tablespoons and adding less icing sugar. It handled well, though – did not run everywhere. Works well on the Chocolate cakes (preceding recipe).

*Tested by:* **Sue Chadwick**

*Frugality and economy are virtues without which no household can prosper. The necessity of economy should be evident to every one, whether in possession of an income barely sufficient for a family's requirements, or of a large fortune which seems to put financial adversity out of the question… Economy and frugality must never, however, be allowed to degenerate into meanness.* (Mrs. Beeton)

# Mrs Gale's Rice Cakes

> 2 oz Butter  ✤  3 oz Caster Sugar  ✤  2 ½ oz Selfraeseing Flour or must
> add a little Baking Powder  ✤  2 ½ oz Rice  ✤  2 eggs well Beaten  ✤  a
> few drops of Lemon or Vinellea
>
> Beat Butter & Sugar to a cream then add Flour Rice & eggs alteranately, bake
> in Patty tins about 10 minutes.  If Rose Cakes are wanted must add a little
> Rose water about a teaspoonfull also a little cochineal to make a pale Pink.

2 oz slightly salted butter
3 oz caster sugar
2 ½ oz plain flour
1 teaspoon baking powder
2 ½ oz rice flour
2 eggs well beaten
A few drops of flavouring e.g.
lemon or vanilla essence; or one
teaspoonful of rose water

1. Preset oven to 190°C / 375°F / Gas 5.
2. Grease a bun tray or use bun cases.
3. Cream butter.
4. Add sugar and continue creaming until light and fluffy.
5. Sift together the flour, baking powder and rice flour.
6. Stir in eggs and flour mixture alternately
7. Divide mixture equally between the 12 bun cases.
8. Bake in the centre of the oven for 8-10 minutes; OR, if using a 2-oven Aga, bake in the roasting oven, on slatted shelf placed on floor and cold shelf on 2nd rung from bottom.

*Comments:*  They were well risen after 10 minutes but slightly dry, which is why I suggest you check them after 8 minutes.  The texture was reminiscent of steamed puddings.  Eat them with jam and cream.

*Cooked in:*  **2 oven gas-fired Aga**
*Tested by:*  **Sue Gowman**

# Drop Cakes

2 Tablespoonfull of Flour  🐝  1 oz Sugar & rather less of Butter  🐝  1 Tablespoonfull of Currents  🐝  1 egg & a little Baking Powder.

Mix as usual & drop on Paper.

1 oz sugar
1 oz butter
3 oz Self-Raising flour
1 egg
1 tablespoon of currants

1. Preheat the oven to 200°C / 400°F / Gas 6.
2. Cream the sugar and butter together.
3. Add the flour and egg and mix well.
4. Add the currants and mix well.

5. Drop teaspoonfuls of mixture onto a greased baking tray.
6. Cook for 8-10 minutes. (Makes about 10)

*Comments:* Make sure you leave a good gap between each dollop on the baking tray because they do spread out rather. They taste like a cross between a rock cake and a biscuit! Unusual texture but very tasty.

*Cooked in:* **Gas oven**
*Tested by:* **Tina Green**

🕊 *The cook is queen of the kitchen; and if she be clean, neat, orderly and quick in her work, those who are under her will emulate these good qualities; upon her the whole responsibility of the kitchen rests, whilst the duty of others is to render her ready and willing assistance.* (Mrs. Beeton) 🕊

# Mrs Meyrick's German Shortbread

¼ lb hot butter stirred with 4 whole eggs into a smooth Paste then ½ lb of Castor sugar & spice either finely Chopped Vanillia or the Grated rind of a Lemon or Cinemon or pounded cloves then about ½ lb of Flour stirred into it then spread it in spoonfulls on a Baking Sheet when has previously been greased then strewn with sliced almonds & sugar. Cut into long stripes before removing from tin.

4 oz butter
4 eggs
8 oz caster sugar

*Choice of flavouring:*
½ teaspoon of ground cinnamon OR grated lemon rind OR finely chopped vanilla (or ½ teaspoon vanilla essence) OR crushed cloves

8 oz plain flour
½ teaspoon mixed spice
2 oz flaked almonds

1. Pre-heat oven to 170°C / 325° F / Gas 3.
2. Grease a baking tray (14 x 9 inch).
3. Melt the butter.
4. Beat the eggs and stir together to make a smooth mix.
5. Stir in castor sugar and mixed spice.
6. Add your choice of flavouring.
7. Stir in the flour and mixed spice a little at a time until it is all incorporated, then beat the mixture for a few minutes.
8. Sprinkle the base of the baking tray with caster sugar and flaked almonds.
9. Spread the mixture onto the tray and bake in the oven for 20 minutes or until golden brown.

*Comments:* This is a very quick and easy recipe, and good to eat. The result is a flat, closely textured cake rather than a biscuit although it does look a bit like shortbread when it is cut into strips. In any case, it has a distinct, sweet, almond taste with a more subtle cinnamon/lemon/ vanilla flavour depending on the choice. Keeps well in an air-tight container for a few days. I have not tested the cloves-flavoured version.

Cooked in: **Electric fan oven**
Tested by: **Alison Baud**

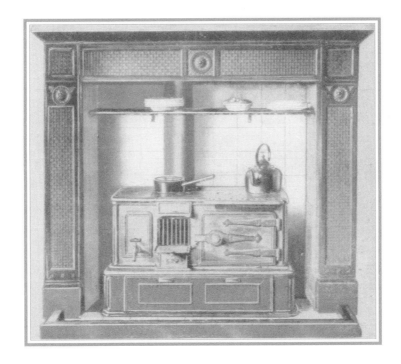

Kitchen ranges may be distinguished as close and open, the chief point of difference between them being in the construction of the fire-grate or box in which the fuel used for heating purposes is burnt... Close ranges are now chiefly used, but open ranges are to be met with in the country and in some towns in the North and in houses that have been built for some years, and in which the open range that was originally fixed in the kitchen, still remains... It may be said, however, that economy of fuel and cleanliness are the chief features of close ranges of all kinds, combined with efficiency of action...  (Mrs. Beeton)

# Scones

1 lb Flour  🐝  3 oz Butter  🐝  1 large Teaspoon Baking Powder  🐝  a little salt  🐝  milk to mix into dough

Rub the Butter into flour add B.P. & Salt mix with milk & roll out ½ an inch thick & bake 20 minutes in a quick oven.

3 oz butter
1 lb Self-Raising flour
1 large teaspoon baking powder
pinch of salt
7 fl oz milk

1. Preheat oven to 190°C / 375°F / Gas 5.
2. Put butter, flour, baking powder and salt into a bowl and mix well with electric mixer.
3. Add milk, and mix up into a dough.
4. Roll out to ½ inch thick and cut into rounds.  Makes about 15 scones.
5. Bake for 9 minutes.  Watch them carefully!
6. Cool, split into halves and butter.

*Comments:*  My first attempt with plain flour turned out very dry.  The second attempt using Self-Raising flour and baking powder was altogether different – much lighter.

*Cooked in:*  **Electric fan oven**
*Tested by:*  **Linda Jordan**

*A good cook has every reason to magnify the office she holds, for her work influences not only the comfort but also the health of the whole household, and mindful of this responsibility she will take care to study both the needs and tastes of those whose food she prepares.*
(Mrs. Beeton)

# Lottie's Doughnuts

Half fill a deep Saucepan with fat line a shallow tin with greased paper. Sift together 3 cupfulls of flour ¾ tea spoonful of Salt 1 teaspoonful of Nutmeg and 4 teaspoonfuls of Baking Powder. Cream ⅔ cup of Castor Sugar with 3 tablespoonful of Butter add half dry ingredients then add 1 beaten egg then ⅔ of cupful of milk add the other Ingredients roll out ½ inch thick cut into rounds of breads brown in a minute it is just hot enough.

12 oz Self-Raising flour
¾ teaspoon salt
1 teaspoon nutmeg
2 teaspoons baking powder
3 oz caster sugar
2 oz butter
1 egg beaten
4 fluid oz milk
2-3 oz Self-Raising flour as required to make dough rollable

1. Mix all dry ingredients together.
2. In a separate bowl cream together butter and sugar.
3. Add half dry ingredients.
4. Add beaten egg and milk a little at a time.
5. Add rest of dry ingredients and beat until smooth.
6. Add more flour if necessary to make it easier to roll out and then put in fridge for at least half an hour.
7. Flour rolling pin and pastry board and roll out dough until about half-inch thick.
8. Switch on deep-fat fryer and heat fat to temperature of 160°C.
9. Using scone cutter, cut out rounds (at least 12), and use smaller circumference cutter to cut out middle of dough, leaving ring-shaped doughnut. This helps to cook the doughnut in the middle.
10. Place 4-5 doughnut rings in deep-fat fryer, turning after 1 minute (max).
11. Lift basket after 1 further minute.
12. Douse in caster sugar – and eat warm!

*Comments:*    Using Lottie's basic ingredients the dough is too wet to roll, so gradually add more flour once all other ingredients have been added.  On one attempt I added the milk to the beaten butter and sugar before the dry ingredients and the mixture curdled, so the next time I added the dry ingredients beforehand and all was fine.  On another attempt I whizzed it all up in the Magimix – there was no curdling but I have to say the hand-mixed batter turned out much lighter.

Either way they are absolutely delicious.  Taste-tested and warmly approved by Rode cricket team!

*Cooked in:*  **Deep-fat fryer**
*Tested by:*  **Alex Sing**

*Do not be afraid of hot water in washing up dishes and dirty cooking utensils; as these are essentially greasy, luke-warm water cannot possibly have the effect of cleansing them thoroughly, and soda in the water is a great saving of time as is also a fresh supply of hot water.*  (Mrs. Beeton)

*After washing the plates and dishes wash out your dish tubs with a little soap, soda and water, and scrub them often; wash the dish cloth also and wring it out, and after wiping out the tubs stand them to dry.*  (Mrs. Beeton)

*Pudding cloths and jelly bags should have immediate attention after being used; the former should be well washed, scalded and hung up to dry.  Let them be perfectly aired before being put away.  No soda should be used in washing pudding cloths.*  (Mrs. Beeton)

# Rose and Lottie

Rose Stratton was Mary Jane's older sister. She was great friends with Charlotte 'Lottie' Giddings, who were their first cousin once removed. They grew up in neighbouring villages, Alton Barnes and Woodborough, and were of similar age despite being of different generations. They went into service together, for in 1901, both Rose and Lottie were working at 14 Foster Road, Alverstoke, near Gosport. Rose was cook, and Lottie housemaid to Dr. Jonathan Kealy and his family.

*Lottie Lee*

Later, Rose met and married a soldier called Arthur Warburton, and Lottie too married a soldier by the name of Lee. Perhaps they met their future husbands when they were working together in Hampshire. Certainly, all four knew each other when they were courting, for Mary Jane used to say that Rose and Lottie had 'married the wrong husbands', that Arthur had been in love with Lottie and Lottie's husband in love with Rose. Mary Jane once told her daughter Marjorie that Lottie's husband came to her in tears one day saying that he wished he had married Rose.

Who knows why this happened? Family tradition does not say. Times being what they were, they all had to live with the situation, and Rose settled down with Arthur and had two children, Arthur and Irene. Lottie and her husband had no children, and how she fared otherwise in her marriage we do not know, but Mary Jane must have thought kindly of her, for she kept her photograph with the other family memorabilia.

Mary Jane collected several recipes from her sister Rose, and two of her cakes are included here, along with the very fine doughnut recipe from her friend Lottie.

# Rose's Sultana Cake

1 lb Sultanas 🌱 1 lb Peel 🌱 1 ½ flour 🌱 4 eggs 🌱 ½ pt milk
🌱 ¾ Butter 🌱 1 crystall sugar 🌱 1 ½ teaspoonfull of Baking
Powder 🌱 A few almonds on top.

Cream Butter & Sugar.  Bake 2 or 3 hours.

6 oz butter or margarine
8 oz brown sugar
2 large eggs
5 fl. oz milk
12 oz Self-Raising flour
8 oz sultanas
8 oz candied peel
Flaked almonds for the top

1.  Preheat the oven to 190°C / 375°F / Gas 5.
2.  Grease and line a 7½-inch round cake tin.
3.  Dust the fruit with flour.
4.  Cream the butter and the sugar.
5.  Beat in the eggs a little at a time, then the milk.  The mixture does curdle, but this doesn't seem to matter.
6.  Fold in the flour.
7.  Fold in the fruit.
8.  Turn the mixture into cake tin, and sprinkle the almonds on top.
9.  Bake for 1 – 1¼ hours, testing at 1 hour; OR for about 2 hours in Aga.

*Comments:*  Half the original quantity makes a large cake – it filled my largest cake-tin.

First attempt: I used brown sugar and forgot the almonds. Went down well (especially with the baby!). Also tested on the SAPPHIRE Project team meeting – 'Fine cake' according to the minutes.  It kept fairly well, but had disappeared within a few days so I can't comment on its long-term properties.

Second attempt with caster sugar: also good (Simon still a fan) but there was a general vote in favour of the brown sugar version.  The almonds on top make it something special.

*Cooked in:* **Aga**
*Tested by:* **Helen Williams**

# Rose's Pound Cake

1 lb flour 🌾 ½ lb Butter 🌾 ½ [lb] Castor Sugar 🌾 ½ Currents 🌾
½ Sultanas 🌾 ½ Peel 🌾 ½ Glaze Cherries 🌾 4 eggs

3 hrs.

8 oz butter
8 oz caster sugar
4 eggs
1 lb plain flour
8 oz currants
8 oz sultanas
8 oz candied peel
8 oz glacé cherries

1. Preheat the oven to 150°C / 300°F / Gas 2.
2. Line an 8-inch round cake tin with greaseproof paper.
3. Cream fat and sugar together until pale and fluffy.
4. Add eggs a little at a time, beating well after each addition.
5. Mix the fruit and flour together.
6. Fold fruit and flour into the creamed mixture.
7. Turn mixture into the tin, and level the top.
8. Bake in the centre of oven for about 2 ½ hours, or until cooked through.
9. Turn out to cool on a wire rack.

*Comments:* A very soft, moist mixture. Keep cake in an airtight tin. The tasters all agreed the cake was delicious.

*Cooked in:* **Gas oven**
*Tested by:* **Verity Smith**

# German Pound Cake

½ lb Butter ❧ 10 oz Flour ❧ ½ lb Sifted Sugar ❧ 3 oz Currents ❧ 3 oz Sultanas ❧ 2 oz Candid Peel ❧ Grated rind of 1 Lemon ❧ 4 eggs

Beat Butter & sugar to a cream then add eggs then flour alteranately. Mix as you put in then add fruit & other Ingredients well mix put in tin & bake 2 hrs in a quick oven.

8 oz butter
8 oz caster sugar
4 eggs, beaten
10 oz plain flour, sifted
3 oz currants
3 oz sultanas
2 oz candied peel
Grated rind of 1 lemon

1. Preset oven to 180° / 350°F / Gas 4.
2. Grease and line an 8-inch loose bottomed round cake tin with baking parchment.
3. Cream the softened butter with the sugar until light and fluffy.
4. Add the eggs and sifted flour alternately.
5. Fold in any remaining flour.
6. Add currants, sultanas, peel and lemon rind, and mix well.
7. Turn out into the prepared cake tin.
8. Bake for 1 hr 50 minutes.

*Comments:* This is a really light, citrus-flavoured fruit cake. Don't use ready-chopped candied peel, but buy the sort you have to chop yourself – it gives a much better flavour.

*Cooked in:* **Conventional electric oven**
*Tested by:* **Sue Chadwick**

# Mrs Parker's Norwich Cake

1 lb Flour 🐝 ½ lb Butter 🐝 1 lb Currents 🐝 ¼ lb Brown Sugar 🐝 ¼ lb Candid Peal 🐝 1 tea spoonfull of mixed spice 🐝 2 tea spoonfull of Baking Powder 🐝 ½ pt Milk

Mix well & bake in a moderate oven 3 hr or longer.

1 lb plain flour
8 oz butter
1 lb currants
4 oz brown sugar
4 oz candied peel (not ready chopped)
1 teaspoons mixed spice
2 teaspoons baking powder
10 fl. oz milk

~∞~

1. Preheat oven to 170°C / 325°F / Gas 3.
2. Grease and line an 8-inch round cake tin.
3. Rub butter into flour.
4. Mix in all other dry ingredients.
5. Make a well in the centre and stir in the milk until it is well mixed.
6. Turn out into prepared tin.
7. Cook for 2 ½ hours in centre of the oven. If you are not using a fan oven you might need to cook it a little longer.

*Comments:* I cooked this in a round tin, but it would probably be better in a loaf tin. I followed the method for tea bread, rubbing butter into flour rather than creaming. The cake has a crunchy crust, but is very moist inside with a lovely flavour. I think this was because I used proper candied peel rather than the pre-chopped sort.

*Cooked in:* **Electric fan oven**
*Tested by:* **Sue Chadwick**

# Fruit Cake

6 oz Flour  ❧  2 eggs  ❧  4 oz Butter  ❧  4 oz Sugar  ❧  Fruit any kind

First beat Butter to a cream with Sugar then add yolk of well beaten eggs whip
the whites to a stiff froth & add by degrees with flour the fruit last with a
teaspoon of B. Powder & well beaten & bake.

4 oz butter
4 oz dark brown sugar
2 eggs
6 oz plain flour
5 oz mixed fruit
1 teaspoon baking powder

❧

1. Preheat oven to 180°C / 350° F / Gas 4.
2. Grease and line a 7-inch round cake tin.
3. Cream butter and sugar together until pale and fluffy.
4. Add well-beaten egg yolks.
5. Whip egg whites until a stiff froth.
6. Add whites very gradually, together with flour, to the mixture.
7. Mix in fruit together with baking powder.
8. Turn out into prepared tin.
9. Bake in centre of oven for 40 minutes; OR, in main oven of Aga with plain shelf above for 40 minutes.

*Cooked in:* **Aga**
*Tested by:* **Sue Chadwick**

# 6
# Chutneys & Preserves

❧

P ickles may now be purchased in such variety and so cheaply that very few, save those who grow vegetables they cannot utilize in any other way, think of preparing them at home.  Pickles consist of vegetables and fruits steeped in vinegar previously boiled with spices, to which is frequently added salt and sugar, in quantities varied according to individual taste...  Indian pickles form a class by themselves; they are generally thick and highly spiced, mangoes forming a general base.

*Mrs Beeton (1907), p.1129*

Mary Jane worked in two households belonging to officers of the Bengal staff corps, so it is not suprising that there are so many chutney recipes in her receipt-book – she has four different recipes for tomato chutney alone! Chutney is a Hindi word, used, as Mrs Beeton tells us, of the mango-based pickles from that part of the world.  Mary Jane's chutneys contain hot spices, but apples, tomatoes and even beetroot replace mangoes as the main ingredient.

I had never made chutneys before tackling some of Mary Jane's receipts, and I was genuinely surprised to find how easy they are to make. Now, as in 1907, there are many commercially-made chutneys and pickles available, but there is no doubt that the home-made variety is spicier, thicker and tastier, with the added advantage of having no chemical additives.

Those of you who, like me, don't have a preserving pan, may like to do as I did and use a wok. It's a wide and shallow pan, and does the job very well.

*The cleaning of the kitchen, passages, and kitchen stairs must always be over before breakfast, so that it may not interfere with the other business of the day. Everything should be ready, and the whole house should wear a comfortable aspect.* (Mrs. Beeton)

*"A place for everything, and everything in its place," must be the rule, in order that time may not be wasted in looking for things when they are wanted, and that the whole business of cooking may move with the regularity and precision of a well-adjusted machine.* (Mrs. Beeton)

# Apple Chutney

2 lbs Hard apples peeled & cored & cut small   🌿   1 lb Brown Sugar   🌿
4 oz Table Salt   🌿   ½ lb stoned & Bruised Raisens   🌿   ½ Ground ginger
🌿   a few dried chillies.

Add enough boiling Vinegar to make into a pulp keep the jar in a warm
place & stir the mixture every day for a month then cover & make airtight.

2 lb prepared cooking apples
(peeled, cored and chopped)
1 lb soft brown sugar
2 teaspoons table salt
8 oz raisins
½ oz ground ginger
a sprinkling of dried chillies
1 pint malt vinegar

1. In a preserving pan put all the dry ingredients and the apples.
2. Pour over the vinegar and mix well.
3. Bring mixture to a gentle simmer and continue simmering, un-covered, stirring regularly, until the vinegar has reduced and the mixture has reached the con-sistency of chutney (a wooden spoon drawn across the base of the pan should leave a clear trail that does not immediately fill up).
4. Remove from the heat, cover the pan, and set aside. If you have the time and patience, stir every day for 1-2 weeks.
5. Bottle in clean jars, cover with waxed discs, and seal with a lid. Leave in a cool place to mature for at least three months before using.

*Comments:* Being completely inex-perienced when it came to chutney-making, I had a disaster with the first batch I made, because I followed Mary Jane's quantities and put in 4 oz table salt. I think she must have made a mistake when she transcribed the recipe into her book, and perhaps she meant 4 *teaspoons* of salt! Anyway, I checked a few apple chutney recipes, and then made the second batch using just 2 teaspoons of table salt.   The result was 3 lbs of sweet, luscious apple chutney.

*Cooked in:*  **Wok on electric hob**
*Tested by:*  **Katy Jordan**

# Hot Tomato Chutney

2 lbs of Tomatoes Ripe or unripe, half them add 2 large onions sliced fine & 6 chillies. Sprinkle with Salt. Fill up with Vinegar to cover them. Boil slowly till the pulp Seperates easily from the skins. Stir the whole through a colunder then take
1 desert spoonfull of Mustard 🐝 1 desert spoonfull of Peper 🐝 1 desert spoonfull Mixed Spice 🐝 ½ lb Demera Sugar 🐝 & boil up again.

2 lbs tomatoes, halved
2 large onions, finely sliced
6 birdeye chillies
2 teaspoons salt
12 fl oz white wine vinegar
2 teaspoons whole mustard
2 teaspoons ground black pepper
2 teaspoons mixed spice
8 oz Demerara sugar

❧

1. Put tomatoes, onions and chillies in a pan, sprinkle with salt and add vinegar to cover. The quantity of vinegar may vary from that given above depending on the size of your pan.
2. Bring to the boil and simmer gently until the tomatoes are cooked and pulpy.
3. Using a metal sieve, strain the mixture well and keep the liquid, using a spoon to push as much of the liquid (and fine pulp) through as possible.
4. Add the spices and sugar to the liquid, and bring to the boil again, stirring constantly.
5. Boil the mixture until it reaches a good set (a wooden spoon drawn across the base of the pan should leave a clear trail that does not immediately fill up).
6. Pot in clean, sterilised jars and leave to mature for a month.

*Comments:* An excellent hot chutney! Since the chutney is sieved and smooth, I chose to use mustard seed rather than powder to give it a little texture. Mustard powder would make an even more fiery chutney (it's pretty hot already), so this was probably a good choice.

    Goes extremely well with mature cheddar.

*Cooked on:* **Electric hob**

*Tested by:* **Nick Gibbins**

1. Tart Pans. 2. Patty Pans. 3. Raised Pie Mould. 4. Paste Jagger. 5. Fancy Vegetable Cutters and Case. 6. Vegetable Scoops. 7. Paste Board and Pin. 8. Plain Charlotte Pudding Mould. 9. Gridiron. 10. Mangle or Wringer. 11. Tin-lined Wicker Knife Basket. 12. Coffee Canister. 13. Bread Grater.

# Sweet Tomato Chutney

Peel 12 large tomatoes mash with a wooden spoon put them in a preserving pan with ¾ lb of white sugar, ¾ lb of Raisens stoned & chopped 2 oz Garlic chopped 2 desertspoonful of ground ginger 3 pts of Vinegar boil & stir for 2 ½ hours.  Put into dry bottles & cork.

2 lb tomatoes
8 oz granulated sugar
8 oz raisins
1½ oz garlic, crushed
2 heaped teaspoons ground ginger
2 pints malt vinegar

1. Blanch the tomatoes in a saucepan of boiling water for 2 minutes, to loosen the skins.
2. Peel off tomato skins and mash the tomatoes in a bowl.
3. Put tomatoes into a preserving pan with the sugar, raisins, garlic, ginger and vinegar.
6. Bring mixture to a gentle simmer and continue simmering, uncovered, stirring regularly, until the vinegar has reduced and the mixture has reached the consistency of chutney (a wooden spoon drawn across the base of the pan should leave a clear trail that does not immediately fill up).
4. Pour into sterilised, hot jars, cover with waxed disc and cap tightly.

*Comments:* The reduced quantities above will make three pounds of beautiful, sweet tomato chutney. Even very new it tastes delicious, and I expect it to improve with keeping.

*Cooked in:* **Wok on electric hob**
*Tested by:* **Katy Jordan**

# Mrs Felce's Green Tomato Chutney

Slice 5 lbs Green Tomatoes into an earthenware pan, sprinkle salt over each layer, set stand 12 hours. Drain off water put slices into an enamelled sauce-pan. Pour over them

1 quart white Vinegar ❧ ¾ Dem. Sugar ❧ ½ lb Sliced Onion ❧ ¼ oz Cloves ❧ ¼ oz bruised ginger root ❧ ¼ oz Capsicun ❧ ¼ mustard seed ❧ very little sharlot ❧ very little garlic

Simmer all stiring occasionally with a wooden spoon untill the Tomatoe is soft then bottle.

---

5 lbs green tomatoes, sliced
12 oz Demerara sugar
8 oz onion, sliced
¼ oz ground cloves
¼ oz ground ginger
¼ oz cayenne pepper
¼ oz mustard seeds
2 shallots, chopped
2 garlic cloves, crushed

❧

1. Layer the green tomatoes in a wide shallow dish, sprinkle with salt between each layer, cover, and leave to stand overnight.

2. Pour off any liquid that has been drawn out of the tomatoes.

3. Put tomatoes and all other dry ingredients into a preserving pan, and pour over the vinegar.

4. Bring to boiling point, then simmer, stirring as required, until the vinegar has reduced and the mixture has reached the consistency of chutney (a wooden spoon drawn across the base of the pan should leave a clear trail that does not immediately fill up).

5. Pour into hot sterilised jars, cover with a waxed disc and cap tightly.

*Comments:* This is a hot, spicy chutney, excellent for using up those leftover green tomatoes at the end of the season.

*Cooked in:* **Wok on electric hob**

*Tested by:* **Katy Jordan**

## Mrs Felce

Mrs. Felce was born Hilda Stratton, one of the eight daughters of Frank and Jane Stratton, who farmed the land around the family home at Manor Farm in Manningford Bohune, Wiltshire. The family seem to have links with the Winchester and Southampton area, for at the time of her marriage in 1908, the 22-year-old Hilda was living at 20 West Hill in Winchester; and she was married at Christ Church, Winton, Bournemouth.

Hilda's new husband was Gilbert Carlyon Felce, the son of Stamford Felce, a physician and surgeon from Paddington, London. Gilbert was an insurance underwriter, who lived and worked in London. At the time of their marriage he was living at 63, Claverton Street in London S.W., just off the Grosvenor Road on the north bank of the Thames in Pimlico. The 1901 census shows the house was at that point inhabited by a family of five with one servant: just the sort of house a young professional man like Gilbert Felce would choose seven years later as his first marital home.

Mary Jane and Hilda Stratton were of very different backgrounds and unlikely to have met socially, but given that they were of an age, and grew up in neighbouring villages, and shared the same surname, it is likely that they knew of each other, at the very least. Perhaps this is why Hilda employed Mary Jane as her cook in London. What Mary Jane made of life in Pimlico we do not know, but she seems to have been on good terms with her employer, and collected several recipes from her. Hilda Felce grew up as a farmer's daughter, and knew all about making preserves and salting down beans!

The Felces clearly maintained their links with Dorset, and owned a farmhouse named Whitecliffe, on Ballard Down above Swanage. In 1935, Hilda Felce loaned Whitecliffe to the artist Paul Nash and his wife, and it was here that Nash worked on the *Shell Guide to Dorset*, writing the text, taking photographs and painting watercolour illustrations. Nash went on to become official War Artist to the Air Ministry during World War II, and in 1941 he painted one of his most famous pictures, 'The Battle of Britain'[1].

[1] Swann, Stephen (2001). In the footsteps of Paul Nash. *Dorset magazine*, 75 (Nov). http://www.dorsetmag.co.uk/magazine/issue075-a0.phtml [accessed 20.7.2003]

# Eva's Beetroot Chutney

2 lbs Beetroot ❧ 1 lb Apples ❧ ½ lb Sugar ❧ 1 Large Onion ❧
½ Pt Vinegar ❧ juice of 1 Lemon ❧ 1 Teaspoonful of Salt ❧ ½
Teaspoonful of Peper.

Boil Beetroot in Salted Water when Cool cut in small cubes. There should be
2 lbs when cooked. Prepare apples & cook 15 minutes with Vinegar Apples
Sugar Lemon Juice & Onion. Season with Salt & Peper add Beetroot & boil
for 5 minutes. Ready for use in 3 days.

2 lbs beetroot cooked weight
1 lb cooking apples, sliced
8 oz granulated sugar
1 large onion, chopped
Juice of 1 lemon
10 fl. oz malt vinegar
1 teaspoon table salt
½ teaspoon pepper

1. Peel the beetroot and boil in salted water until tender OR buy cooked whole beetroot.
2. Cut beetroot into small cubes and set aside.
3. In a preserving pan put the apples, sugar, onion, and lemon juice with the vinegar. Bring to the boil and cook for 15 minutes.
7. Add the beetroot cubes, season with salt and pepper, bring mixture to a gentle simmer and continue simmering, uncovered, stirring regularly, for about 50 minutes, or until the vinegar has reduced and the mixture has reached the consistency of chutney (a wooden spoon drawn across the base of the pan should leave a clear trail that does not immediately fill up).
4. Pour into clean hot jars, cover with waxed discs and seal tightly with a lid.

*Comments:* This makes about 4 lb of chutney, which is ready to eat almost immediately. Great as a relish with salads.

*Cooked in:* **Wok on electric hob**
*Tested by:* **Katy Jordan**

# Eva and her family

E va Hawkins was the eldest child of Mary Jane's half-sister. Letitia Ann Marshall, always known as Annie, was Hannah Marshall's eldest child, born when Hannah was twenty. In 1891, Annie married James Hawkins, a farm labourer from Manningford Bohune, and they soon had three children, Eva, William and Elsie. Then tragedy struck: James died suddenly of appendicitis. This was in the days before the operation for appendicitis had been discovered. Appendicitis was known as 'inflammation of the bowel', and it was a killer. So Eva's mother Annie was left to bring up her three children alone. They were desperately poor, and Annie earned what money she could by taking in washing. Annie's great-niece Rosalind recalls that, whenever she thinks of her Aunt Annie, she sees her up to her elbows in soapsuds. James's sudden death was the first of a series of misfortunes in store for the little family.

Taking in washing made a lot of extra work for Annie, and she couldn't watch Eva's baby brother William all the time. She would leave him sleeping on a bed upstairs while she set to work, and one day he fell off the bed and injured his head badly. The fall caused brain damage that confined him to a wheelchair for the rest of his life. Annie's niece Marjorie firmly believes that if the poor woman had not had so much extra work to do to look after her family, the accident would never have happened. She remembers Will as being very clever with his hands, able to make all kinds of things, although they were twisted up as a result of his injury. He could also play the melodeon beautifully.

Eva herself went into service at a very young age, working for a local well-to-do Stratton family. Family tradition says that they took her into service so young out of kindness, to help out Annie, so that she would have one less mouth to feed. Eva became engaged to a young man who was killed during the First World War. She later married her cousin, Herbert Stratton, and they lived at Honeystreet in one of a pair of cottages beside the lane leading down to the Barge Inn. Bert and Eva had one son, Harold Stratton, born in 1922.

*Eva and Harold*

After her mother Hannah died, Annie went to keep house for her step-father and half-brother, at the family home in Honeystreet, where she was near her married daughter Eva. Eva's son Harold grew up and married Violet Blanche Wiltshire, and soon baby Christine had arrived. A wonderful family photograph shows four generations: Harold, Eva and Annie with Christine on her lap. Annie looks serene in her old age, a gentle matriarch. Sadly, less than 6 months later, baby Christine died suddenly. But Harold and Violet had another child, their daughter Jennifer, who still lives in the Pewsey Vale with her husband.

*Four Generations*

I remember visiting Eva and Bert Stratton in the cottage at Honeystreet, listening to the clock ticking steadily while their budgerigar Joey chirped in his cage. They had a deep well just outside the back door, and an old privy in a shed down the garden. Once when we arrived there was a sheet stretched out on the grass in the front garden, covered with dandelion heads drying in the sun. Eva was making dandelion wine (see p.138). She also made excellent beetroot chutney, and gave her recipe to her young aunt Mary Jane.

# Lady Malcolm's Mincemeat

3 lb apples 🌾 1½ lb Suet 🌾 1½ lb Raisens 🌾 2 lb Currents 🌾
1½ lb Sugar 🌾 2 Lemons Rind & juice 🌾 ½ oz spice 🌾 ¼ oz salt
🌾 Candid Peel 🌾 ¼ pint port 🌾 ¼ pint Brandy

1 lb 8 oz eating apples, finely
chopped or grated
12 oz suet
12 oz raisins
1 lb currants
12 oz granulated sugar
juice and zest of one lemon
¼ oz mixed spices
½ teaspoon salt
1 oz candied peel, finely chopped
2 fl oz brandy
2 fl oz port

❧

1. Grate or finely chop apples, and mix well with all remaining ingredients except for the port and the brandy in a large heat-proof bowl.
2. Cover with cling-film and leave in a cool place for at least 12 hours (and as much as three days) for the flavours to develop.
3. Remove cling-film, cover with aluminium foil and place in a low oven (120°C) for three hours.
4. Stir well, checking that the suet has melted, and when cool add the port and the brandy and stir well again to mix.
5. Pot in clean sterilised jars, cover with a wax disc, cap tightly and leave to mature for a month.

*Comments:* Main tip: use the biggest bowl you own – you'll need it. Even halving the quantities left us with a huge amount.

The method (cooking the mincemeat to melt the suet) is taken from one of Delia Smith's recipes, and is intended to prevent the mincemeat fermenting in the jar.

*Cooked in:* **Conventional electric oven**
*Tested by:* **Nick Gibbins**

# Lady Wilhelmina Charlotte Malcolm

Wilhelmina Charlotte was born c. 1833, the youngest daughter of the Rev. Henry Albright Hughes, of Stoke in Devon. On 19th October 1852, she married Captain George Malcolm of the Indian Army. He was the son of a Bombay merchant, David Malcolm, and his wife Mary. Mary was the daughter of Henry Hughes, and the sister of Wilhelmina's father, so this is how the Indian Army Captain from Bombay came to marry the clergyman's daughter from the west coast of Devon.

George Malcolm was a member of a most remarkable Scottish family. His grandfather, also named George Malcolm, was a sheep-farmer from Dumfriesshire. He and his wife Margaret had 15 children, of which 13 survived: 10 sons and three daughters. Four of the sons reached rank and greatness, entirely through their own efforts: these were Admiral Sir Pulteney Malcolm; Major-General Sir John Malcolm; Sir James Malcolm; and Vice-Admiral Sir Charles Malcolm. Their brother David was the merchant of Bombay whose son followed in his eminent uncles' footsteps, rising through the ranks of the Indian Army to become at last General Sir George Malcolm of the Bombay Staff Corps, and a Knight Commander of the Most Noble Order of the Bath (KCB).

While in the army, General Sir George and Lady Malcolm maintained a London residence at 13, Cromwell Crescent, S.W., and he was a member of the United Services Club and the National Club. When he retired from the army in 1881, they lived at Guys-dale, Leamington Spa, with their daughter Helen and disabled son David, who had been partially paralysed from birth. On 6th April 1897, the General died, leaving his wife the sum of £8923.19s.9d.

So at 64, Wilhelmina Charlotte Malcolm was left a widow with a partially paralysed son and an unmarried daughter to support. By 1901 she had reduced her household by moving to Clevedon, and was living not far from the Old Church at 13 Jesmond Road. Here she had a household staff of three: a cook, a parlour maid, and an under-house maid. By 1904 she had moved around the corner to 5 Jesmond Road, and by 1908 she had moved again around the corner to 'Penshurst', 17 Victoria Road.

Mary Jane worked as cook for Lady Malcolm in Clevedon sometime between 1907 and 1911. Her receipt-book contains several recipes from Lady Malcolm, such as the fine mincemeat included here. She seems to have been a kind and friendly employer, and it may be that, coming herself from a small Devon village, she felt more at home sharing recipes with her country-born cook than taking tea with the pukka officers' wives in Bombay. She died on 13th December 1911, and the remainder of her estate, just £929.3s.9d, went to her eldest son Major Pulteney Malcolm of the India Army.

Mary Jane always retained fond memories of Lady Malcolm, and years later when the family went on holiday to Weston-super-Mare, they made a special trip to Clevedon to look for her grave. They started at the cemetery, and having had no success looking at gravestones, they asked a man who was tidying up if he knew where her grave might be. "Lady Malcolm? She'd be with the upper 'uns," he told them, directing them up to the graveyard around St Andrew's church on the cliff edge. But they couldn't find her grave, and neither could a friend and I fifty years later. The graveyard clerk assures me that nobody of the name of Malcolm is buried there, and so it is most likely that Wilhelmina Charlotte Malcolm lies beside her husband General Sir George at Leamington Spa.

# Other fruit and vegetable preserves

*Here are several other pickles and preserves from Mary Jane's receipt-book that you might like to try.*

## Mrs Woolfrey's Bottled Gooseberries Rhubarb & Damsons

Fill glass Bottles with either of the above & tie down with brown paper. Put them in a large Fish Kettle or Pot or in the oven when the fruit does down about ½ way it is done take out & fill up with boiling water & put Salad oil or Mutton Dripping on top & tie down.

# Mrs Felce's method of preserving French Beans

Pick when quite dry & not very young. Top & Tail & remove hard sides. Use small pan or wide mouthed jar put layer of very dry salt first then the beans & the rest alternately in salt & beans. Quite cover top layer with plenty of salt. Tie down securely. When using wash in 3 waters & will not keep long after opening.

# To Preserve Vegetable Marrow

Peel 1 or more marrow to the weight of 3 lbs. Cut them in quarters & take out the seeds. Put the pieces in cold water for 12 hrs. Drain them. Sprinke with ½ lb of moist sugar & let them stand for 12 hrs. Cut the marrow into small pieces about an inch square, put them into a pan on the fire, add 3 lbs of loaf sugar, 1 pt of Water, the juice & pulp of 2 Lemons. Add 2 oz of bruised ginger, & the peel of the Lemons tied up in a muslin bag which should be taken out when it is finished. Boil gently ½ hr. Pour into wide mouth glass Bottles, must begin early about 9 o'clock in the morning so as to allow plenty of time.

# Mrs Smith's Pickled Marrow

Cut Marrow into small squares & cover with Salt over night. Drain it to every 4 lbs add 2 pts Vinegar 6 chillies 6 cloves ½ oz Temeric ½ oz Mustard a breadfast cup of brown Sugar. Tie this in a piece of Muslin & boil in the Vinegar 20 minutes then take it out add the Marrow in the boiling Vinegar & let boil for 20 minutes.

# 7

# Jams, Jellies & Marmalades

❦

**M**armalades and jams are now so cheap that they are within reach of the poorest. They can also be bought so good that there is little inducement to make them at home if the fruit has to be bought or is dear. Nevertheless, it must be confessed that they are seldom both cheap and good, so that housekeepers who desire both quality and economy, and are not over-anxious to spare their own trouble, usually prefer them home-made.

*Mrs Beeton (1907), p.1127*

This advice from Mrs. Beeton is just as valid 100 years on. Anyone who has tasted home-made jam knows how very much better it is than almost any of the jams you will find on the supermarket shelves. It is not all that time-consuming or troublesome to make, and it is actually better to make it in small quantities, so you need not find your store-cupboards overflowing with preserves. Many of the cakes and puddings in this book call for jam, and several testers advise using home-made preserves, because commercial jams and marmalades are not thick and fruity enough to give good results.

Jam-making was not just something Mary Jane did in service, but was part of her yearly routine. There were fruit-bushes in the garden at Orchard Cottage: black-, white- and red-currants, and gooseberries; and a Victoria plum and Bramley apple tree. Blackberries grew wild on Martinsell hilltop and in the hedgerows (as they still do). When her daughter Marjorie went away on holiday in the late 1940s, Mary Jane wrote to her: "Miss Kemm charged 10/- for 4 lb of Raspberries. Mrs Watson helped string the Currants. We are making jam tonight."

*If you live in the country have your vegetables gathered from the garden at an early hour, so that there is ample time to get rid of caterpillars, etc., which is an easy task if the greens are allowed to soak in salt and water an hour or two.* (Mrs. Beeton)

*Punctuality. – This is an indispensable quality in a cook. When there is a large dinner to prepare get all you can done the day before or early on the morning of the day. This will save a great deal of time and enable you, with good management, to send up your dinner in good time and style.* (Mrs. Beeton)

*When you have washed your saucepans, fish kettle, etc., stand them before the fire for a few minutes to get thoroughly dry inside before putting away. They should then be put in a dry place in order to escape rust.* (Mrs. Beeton)

# Apricot Jam

1 lb Dryed Apricots  ❧ 5 lb sugar  ❧ 4 quarts water

Soak the Apricots 24 hrs in the water boil for ½ an hour.  Add the sugar &
boil ¾ hr makes about 12 lb of jam.

12 oz dried apricots
2 pints water
2 lbs sugar

❧

1. **Wash the apricots, cut them into small pieces, cover with the water and soak for 24 hours.**
2. **Turn the fruit and remaining water into the preserving pan and bring gently to boiling point.**
3. **Add the sugar.  Stir over low heat until the sugar is dissolved, then boil for 1 hour.**
4. **Remove from the heat, and skim if necessary.**
5. **Pour into hot jars and allow to cool.**
6. **Cover and seal up jam.**

*Comments:* This recipe shows how much some cooking ingredients have changed in 100 years.

For our first attempt at the jam we halved Mary Jane's ingredients, but otherwise followed her method exactly.  The result was very sugary and tasted more like toffee.  It only produced about 2½ lbs jam, less than half the amount we were expecting.

We think that the apricots she used would have been much drier, and probably also less sugary, than the ones we have today.  They would swell up far more when soaked, and need more sugar to make into palatable jam.  This is why our quantities of ingredients are so different from hers.  They still make a very sweet jam, as we think hers would have been.

*Cooked on:* **Gas hob**
*Tested by:* **Christine Clist and Rachel-Mary Perry**

# Blackberry Jam

½ lb Apples to 1 lb Blackberries & ¾ lb Sugar.

1 lb blackberries
12 oz granulated sugar
8 oz cooking apple (sliced weight)

༄

1. Put the blackberries and sugar together in your preserving pan, mix lightly together and leave overnight, covered.
2. Put a tea-plate into the freezer to chill.
3. Bring gently to simmering point and simmer very gently until the sugar is dissolved in blackberry juice.
4. Add the sliced apple and continue simmering until the jam reaches the point where it will set. Test by putting one teaspoon of jam onto a cold plate, wait a few seconds, then push your finger through it. If it leaves the surface clean and forms wrinkles on the surface, it is done.
5. Pour immediately into sterilised hot jars, cover with a waxed disc and seal.

*Comments:* Made with hedgerow blackberries and Bramley apples, this jam is a real taste of harvest-time.

*Cooked in:* **Wok on electric hob**
*Tested by:* **Katy Jordan**

*Whilst a cook should be versed in all the details of her position, a mistress should never forget her own duty of seeing that the laws of economy, cleanliness and order are not neglected by her servants. The servants who reflect that some day they will probably need neatness, cleanliness and economy in their own homes, and for their own benefit, will feel grateful to the employer who insists on the practice of these virtues.* (Mrs. Beeton)

# Ginger Rhubarb

2 oz ground ginger ❧ 2 Lemons juice & rind ❧ 12 lbs of Rhubarb ❧ 12 lbs of sugar.

Put all together in a baisen leave it for 12 hrs all night. It should be covered. Bring it to the boil & allow it to boil ½ an hour. Put a tea spoonful on a plate to see if it will set if not a little longer.

3 lbs rhubarb
½ oz ground ginger
3 lbs granulated sugar
juice and zest of half a lemon

1. Trim rhubarb and cut into 1-inch pieces.
2. Mix ground ginger with sugar, and layer with rhubarb in a large bowl, adding lemon juice and zest to each layer.
3. Cover bowl with cling-film and leave in a cool place overnight. The lemon juice and sugar will draw out juices from the rhubarb. After resting overnight, the mixture should consist of softened pieces of rhubarb in a thick syrup.
4. Put mixture in a large pan, bring to boil, and boil rapidly for 15 minutes, so that the rhubarb pieces begin to soften and break down.
5. Keep mixture boiling until it reaches the point when it will set. Test by putting one teaspoon of jam onto a cold plate, wait a few seconds, then push your finger through it. If it leaves the surface clean and forms wrinkles on the surface, it is done.
6. Pot in clean sterilised jars, and leave to mature for a month.

*Comments:* The taste is good. I recommend using more lemon juice (1 lemon per 3 lbs of rhubarb) than was called for in Mary Jane's recipe, which should slightly improve the final set (pectin in the zest) and add some needed sharpness to the taste. I left the jam to mature for a month, which may have been slightly more than was necessary. The only spoilage was from a jar that wasn't completely filled (and so was to be expected) – not mouldy, but slightly musty-smelling.

*Cooked on:* **Conventional electric hob**

*Tested by:* **Nick Gibbins**

Mayonnaise Mixer, Mincer, Asparagus Dish, Masher and Strainer, Egg Foiler, Table Hot Plate, Hot Water Dish, Gas Grilling Stove, Cream Freezer.

# Apple Jelly

Whipe & stalk any small apples.  Do not peel or core them.  Fill a pot 3 parts full with the apples & add enough water to cover them.  Cook to a pulp then drain through a hair Sieve.  Weigh the juise & to every quart add

1 lb of Sugar ❧ 6 or 7 Cloves ❧ 1 salt spoon of Grated Nutmeg ❧ & a little stick Cinnamen tied in Muslin then pared Rind & juice of Lemon. Boil the whole untill it thickens.  Strain juice & bottle.

3 lb cooking apples
water to cover
1 lb sugar
7 cloves
½ teaspoon ground nutmeg
½ teaspoon ground cinnamon
zest and juice of 1 lemon

1. Put a tea-plate into the freezer to chill.
2. Wash the apples, then roughly chop them into a large saucepan.
3. Cover with water, bring to a boil and cook them until the apples are reduced to pulp.
4. Strain apple pulp through a colander or large sieve lined with muslin to extract the juice.
5. Measure two pints of the apple juice to make your jelly.
6. Put apple juice, sugar, spices and lemon zest and juice into a preserving pan.
7. Bring to simmering point, stirring well to dissolve sugar.
8. Simmer, stirring regularly, until it will set.  Test by putting one teaspoon of jam onto a cold plate, wait a few seconds, then push your finger through it.  If it leaves the surface clean and forms wrinkles on the surface, it is done.
9. Pour into clean hot jars, cover with a waxed disc and seal immediately.

*Comments:* This makes about two pounds of honey-coloured, spicy, sweet apple jelly.

*Cooked in:* **Wok on electric hob**
*Tested by:* **Katy Jordan**

# Gooseberry Jelly

> To every quart of berries allow 1 pt of water. To every pt of Juice allow 1 lb sugar. Stew the berries in the amount of water till the fruit is quite broken while hot strain but do not press the fruit. Boil the strained juice with the sugar for 20 minutes or till it will jelly on a plate. It should be a pretty pink colour.

1 lb 11 oz green gooseberries (or fill
a 2-pint jug with fruit)
1 pint water
1 lb granulated sugar

1. Put a plate into the freezer to chill.
2. Pinch out the stems and tails of the gooseberries, and put the fruit into a large saucepan.
3. Pour on the water and stew the fruit until it is broken up. This takes about 5 minutes.
4. Line a plastic sieve with a generous piece of gauze, and strain fruit through this into a bowl. Discard the fruit pulp.
5. Return the liquid to the pan, add the sugar, and stir over a low heat until the sugar is fully dissolved.
6. Bring to the boil, uncovered, and keep at a rolling boil for 20 minutes. The pale green syrup really does gradually – and magically – turn as pink as Turkish Delight.
7. Test for a set by putting one teaspoon of jam onto a cold plate, wait a few seconds, then push your finger through it. If it leaves the surface clean and forms wrinkles on the surface, it is done. Test at 5-minute intervals until you get a good set.
8. Using a jam funnel, pour into clean hot jam-jars, cover immediately with a waxed disc and seal.
9. This quantity makes two pounds of jelly.

*Comments:* Having never made jam or jelly before, I was amazed to find how easy it is. The only tricky part is knowing when the jam will set, and the chilled-plate test is very reliable. There is very little to do in preparing the fruit. The only (literally) painful part was picking the gooseberries. I had forgotten the bushes had thorns, and I came home from the local Pick-Your-Own looking as if my hands and arms had been savaged by an affectionate but delinquent kitten. But it was worth it.

*Cooked in:* **Wok on electric hob**
*Tested by:* **Katy Jordan**

# Actual Experience has proved

*in houses or flats where gas fires and gas cookers are used*

# That One Servant can Do the Work of Two

*as compared with a house in which coal is used ; and that Laundry and Cleaners' bills are reduced ; Carpets, Curtains, Tapestry, Blinds, and Wall-papers last longer ; while the Comfort and Convenience of the household are greatly enhanced.*

*If you are anxious to reduce House-keeping Expenses, and increase Home Comforts, you should write to The Gas Light and Coke Company, Horseferry Road, S.W., for their illustrated pamphlet, "Domestic Problems," or visit one of their showrooms, a list of which will be readily furnished on application.*

# Dundee Marmalade

Take 6 good sized oranges seville. Cut them in slices take out all the seeds but nothing more. Put the pieces with 3 pts of Cold Water & let them remain covered for 24 hrs. Boil steadily & slowly for 2 hrs add 5 lbs of loaf sugar broken small & again boil for 2 hrs or more. If the syrup looks too thin add the juice of 2 Lemons or more according to taste. Instead of adding Lemon juice I always leave out 1 orange & cut up a lemon. It ought to be quite clear & the syrup should stiffen slightly.

5 Seville oranges
1 lemon
3 pints of water
5 lbs granulated sugar

*List of Equipment*
Large pan
Long-handled wooden spoon
Square of muslin
Saucers (for testing for a set)
6 or 7 1lb jars with lids (washed, rinsed and dried)
Wide funnel
Waxed discs

❧

1. Wash the fruit.
2. Cut the oranges and lemon into slices (discs) - as thin as you can manage by hand.
3. Remove the pips and place these in a muslin square, then tie up into a loose bag.
4. Put the pieces into the pan with 3 pints of cold water. Cover with a cloth and leave to soak for 24 hours.
5. Cut fruit roughly into thin shreds and return to the pan. Tie the muslin bag on to the handle of the pan so that it dangles into the water.
6. Now turn on the heat, bring the liquid up to the boil and simmer gently in the open pan for 2 hours.
7. Take out the bag of pips and add the sugar. Stir over a low heat until it is all melted and the syrup is clear.
8. Put the saucers into the freezer.
9. Turn up the heat, squeeze the pip bag into the pan and bring the

mixture up to a fast boil, stirring occasionally.

10. After 15 minutes, put a spoonful of marmalade onto one of the cold saucers and put it into the fridge to cool for a few minutes. The marmalade is set if the surface wrinkles slightly when pushed with a spoon. As Mary Jane puts it, it "ought to be quite clear and the syrup should stiffen slightly".

11. If it does not set immediately keep testing in the same way every five minutes until it does.

12. Remove the pan from the heat and spoon off any scum.

13. Stir and leave to settle for about 15-20 minutes.

14. Heat the jars on a tray in the oven.

15. Pour the marmalade into the jars using the funnel.

16. Put a waxed disc on top of each jar and seal while still hot.

*Comments:* This recipe made seven 1lb jars of beautiful, dark orange, thick, rough-cut marmalade which was delicious, truly home-made and very satisfying to make. It must be noted that the season for Seville oranges is very short, January to February. Marmalade is always best and traditionally made with Seville oranges, but in fact I used large Valencia oranges and it still tasted delicious and not too sweet. I was curious about the quantities specified by Mary Jane as it called for rather less water and more sugar than I would expect. Certainly, she does not specify the actual weight of fruit to use. I used 3-4 lbs of fruit in total and it worked very well. One advantage is the soaking of the fruit overnight which softens the peel even before starting to cook. Mary Jane makes no mention of tying the seeds into a muslin bag but I do this as the seed and pith contain the pectin that helps the marmalade to set. You will note also that I boil the marmalade with the sugar for nearly 2 hours less than Mary Jane. I can only speculate that it is possible to bring the mixture up to a fast boil much quicker on a modern hob using a stainless steel pan. It is not advisable, in any case, to boil marmalade for too long as this can cause it not to set.

*Cooked on:* **Electric hob**
*Tested by:* **Alison Baud**

# Beckhampton Racing Stables

While still quite inexperienced in service, Mary Jane went to work at the racing stables at Beckhampton House, on the London Road near Avebury. The house itself was built during the eighteenth century, and was originally the Catherine Wheel Inn, set up to take advantage of the passing trade at Beckhampton crossroads. By the middle of the nineteenth century, the name had changed to the Beckhampton House Inn, and the publican at that time, William Treen, had begun training racehorses as a sideline. Gradually the racehorse-training took over, and by the time Mary Jane's employer, Sam Darling, became proprietor in 1882, the stables were well-established. Sam remained proprietor until he died in 1921, when his son Fred took over.

Beckhampton House itself was "a comfortable, old-fashioned farmhouse, with a long, low-ceilinged dining room."[1] Sam extended and modernised the house greatly, and diversified into farming, breeding prize-winning sheep and cattle. Most of the stable yard as it is today dates from Sam's time, and here he and his son Fred trained many champion racehorses. Some of these are celebrated in the names of houses nearby: Galteemore, Wildflower (the horse was actually called Wildfowler), and Willonyx.

In 1901, the census shows us the extent of the household and stables. 'Darling House' was home to Sam Darling and his wife Violetta, and their sons Fred (16), already a jockey, and Douglas (6). In the house they had a housemaid, kitchenmaid, nursemaid and lady's help. They also employed a coachman. No cook is listed, but she may have lived out, and there is certainly a cook living in a nearby property. As well as these domestic servants, there were 23 jockeys employed in the stables.

Mary Jane came in the early 1900s to work as kitchenmaid. It seems that someone on the staff – most likely the cook - tried to take advantage of her inexperience and keep her working even longer hours than were required. Few servants had more than one afternoon and evening off per week, but two full months after starting work here, Mary Jane still had not been given any time off. So she got up the courage to ask to see 'the lady', Violetta Darling, who was horrified when she heard what had happened. She gave Mary Jane time off immediately, and took steps to ensure that her new kitchen-maid had her full entitlement of leave in future.

[1] Brunning, Jane (2000). *Beckhampton: a village through time.* Privately published, pp.24

# Lemon Cheese Cake

¼ lb Butter  🍇  1 lb Powdered sugar  🍇  6 eggs  🍇  3 large Lemons

Melt the Butter in a stewpan & when desolved add the sugar the yolkes of 6 eggs & the whites of 4 well beaten the Grated rind & juice of the Lemons stir over the fire till it is as thick as good cream.  Pot & tie down for ordinary use & it will keep for months.

2 oz butter
8 oz caster sugar
3 egg yolks
2 egg whites, well beaten
Grated rind & juice of 1½ lemons

❧

1. Melt the butter in a saucepan.
2. Add the sugar, egg yolks, egg whites and lemon juice and rind.
3. Stir over a gentle heat until it is thick and creamy, and just at boiling point.
4. Allow to cool for 5 minutes.
5. Pour into clean hot jam-jars and allow to cool.
6. Cover with greaseproof rounds, and seal with cellophane.

*Comments:* This is not a cheesecake as we would think of it, but lemon cheese or curd.

It was very quick to make – the longest part was stirring the mixture. I halved the original ingredients, and it made 1½ lbs.

*Cooked on:* **Gas hob**
*Tested by:* **Linda Jordan**

*Clean tin [utensils] with soap and whiting, rubbing on with a soft rag or flannel, wiping them with a dry cloth, and lastly with a soft dry cloth or leather.* (Mrs. Beeton)

# Green Tomato Jam

To every lb of Tomatoes add ¾ lb of perserving Sugar.  Pare thinely Rind of 1
lemon cut off the white & slice the inside of the Lemon removing the pips.  Slice
the Tomatoes & put them with the Sugar & Lemon in the perseving pan.  Boil
untill the Tomatoes are quite Transparent & the whole a good consistency.  Pour
into jam pots & tie down.

*Comments* Here's an untested recipe for you to try.  Not a jam that you will ever find on the supermarket shelves, but an alternative to chutney when you want to use up those green tomatoes at the end of the summer.

*Refrigerators are very necessary in a household, as they ensure both comfort and economy, and, indeed, promote good health in the summer.  They consist essentially of cupboards or chests, lined with zinc, and kept cool by ice...  An ice closet, or refrigerator, should not be kept in a kitchen; place it in the larder, at all events well away from the direct sunlight; choose the darkest corner.* (Mrs. Beeton)

*The treatment of servants is of the greatest importance to both mistress and domestics.  If the latter perceive that their mistress's conduct is regulated by high and correct principles, they will not fail to respect her; and if a real desire is shown to promote their comfort, while at the same time a steady performance of their duty is exacted, then well-principled servants will be anxious to earn approval, and their respect will not be unmingled with affection.* (Mrs. Beeton)

# 8

# Boiled Sweets

◦~∾◦

U ntil recently the art of sweetmeat-making was little understood, and still
less practised, by private individuals. Even now there exists a mistaken
idea that this artistic branch of cookery presents many difficulties, and
that elaborate utensils and implements are essential. . . By measuring
accurately, testing repeatedly, and by taking care to apply the right amount of heat,
an amateur should find no difficulty in preparing any of the sweetmeats for which
recipes are given. . .

*Mrs. Beeton (1907), p.1067*

There is only one boiled sweet recipe in Mary Jane's receipt-book, and that is
for good old-fashioned slab toffee, the sort that used to come in flat trays with
a little hammer so that you can break it up small enough to eat.

# Toffee

¾ lb of Butter  ❧  1 lb granualeted sugar  ❧  ¾ lb Demera  ❧  2 table spoonfull of Vinegar in a breakfast cup of water  ❧  essence of Lemon to taste

Boil ½ an hour stirring well pour into a well buttered tin or dish when cool cut into bars or squares.

12 oz butter
1 lb granulated sugar
12 oz Demerara sugar
2 tablespoons of vinegar in 7 fl. oz
of water

❧

1. Line a 6-inch x 10-inch tin with greaseproof paper.
2. Put all ingredients into a saucepan and stir well.
3. Bring to the boil, and boil at 270°C for 30 minutes, stirring regularly.
4. Pour into the prepared tin.
5. Leave to set for about 30 minutes, then cut into squares.

*Comments:* It's *very* hard! Definitely more sucky toffee than chewy toffee. After about a week it becomes easier to bite. So very tasty but a bit hard on the teeth.

You will need to use a thermometer to get the boiling temperature correct.

*Cooked on:* **Gas hob**
*Tested by:* **Tina Green**

# 9
# Country Wines,
# Beers & Spirits

‿◦‿

**M**rs. Beeton has nothing at all to tell her readers on the subject of country wines. She is, naturally, most informative about fine French and German wines, and how they should be stored, bottled, decanted and served. No other wines are worthy of mention, indeed it would seem that these two countries are the only places in the world where wine is made.

Yet, once past this restrictive introduction, Mrs. Beeton's reader finds a whole section of recipes for country wines and beverages. She knew her public. There is a long and honourable tradition of using orchard and hedgerow fruits and garden vegetables to make wines and beers, and to flavour spiritous liquors.

There is still a great deal of interest in making country wines, and at their best they are both wonderful-tasting and very potent. My father used to make an elderberry wine that could put anyone under the table after a glass or two. He was always looking for new country wine recipes, and so it is for keen wine-makers like him that I am happy to include here all Mary Jane's wine recipes.

We have not tested any of these. Making a good country wine takes time, experience and the right equipment (although a tub and a blanket seem to have worked for Mary Jane).

Besides, I needed my testers to stay sober. . .

# Apple Beer

To every gallon of water add  ✲  2 lb Apples  ✲  1 ½ lbs Sugar  ✲  2 oz
ginger  ✲  ½ teaspoonful of Cinnamon  ✲  ½ tea spoonful of cloves

Rub apples through a Suet Grater add 1 gal of Water to every 2 lb of apples, stir
every day for a fortnight.  Strain, add sugar, ginger, cloves & cinnamon.  Place all
in a Cask & bung up tight.  The Contents can be strained & bottled in about a
month and should taste like good Cider.

# Apple Wine

Put 8 quarts of Crushed Apples and 2 gallons of Water Boiling into a pan, cover
with Blanket and leave 14 days.  Strain, weigh, and add 2 lb pure Cane Sugar to
every pound.  Disolve sugar in the Liquid, pour into large Tub & cover over.  When
the scum has formed on top skim off carefully & leave till following day.  Pour into
bottles, cork & seal.

# Beetroot Wine/Mock Port

Well wash 4 lb of Beetroot cut up quickly as possible into small pieces put into cold
water allowing 4 lb to the Gallon boil until tender & all colour extracted.  Strain, and
to every gal of Liquor add 3 lb of Sugar the juice of a Lemon a small piece of Ginger
& a few cloves.  A handful of Raisens to each gal will greatly improve the Wine.  Stir
well untill the Sugar is dissolved & when cold place in Cask adding a piece of
Toasted bread covered with yeast bung tightly when fermentation ceases.

# Blackberry Wine

Bruise 10 lb of sound Blackberries put into a Tub add 2 gals of cold water cover
with a Cloth leave for 3 days strain through a Muslin bag pressing the pulp well
return the juice to the tub add 6 lb of loaf Sugar stir until dissolved cover & leave
2 weeks pour into a dry Cask bung closely & leave 12 months.

# Blackcurrant Wine

### To every gal. water
2 lb Currents    4 lb Sugar

Remove the stalks from Currants put into earthenware bowl press them well & strain off the Juice. To the juice add sugar & water to make a gallon extract a little of the juice & put into Basin with a dessertspoonful of Yeast, allow this to ferment until the Yeast gets to the top of the baisen, add to other juice. At the end of 24 hrs the whole should be fermented, put into Cask & allow to remain until fermentation ceases which will be 14 days then draw from Cask & strain though Muslin, put all back into Cask. If not sweet enough add ½ lb sugar to the gal. The wine should be ready in 3 months.

# Carrot Wine

Boil 7 lb of Carrots in 4 gals of Water until soft but not mushy. Strain off the liquor & add 10 or 12 lb of Sugar. Boil for an hour skiming the while & when cooled down add 2 Tablespoon of Yeast spread on Toast. Let it stand for 10 days stiring every day & skim put in Cask & close for 6 to 12 months. Beetroot & Carrot best made in the Autumn.

# Damson Wine

### To every gal of water
2 ½ lb of Damsons    3 lb sugar.

Bruise the Damsons break a few stones, so that the nuts flavour the wine soak the Damsons 24 hours press all strain away the Liquor, to this Liquor add sugar. Extract a little of the juice & put into a basin with a desert-spoonful of Yeast allow this to ferment, until the Yeast gets to the top of the baisen, then add to other juice. At the end of 24 hours the whole should be fermented and put in a cask & allow to remain 14 days then draw from Cask & strain the remains through a Muslin bag. Put back into the cask. If not sweet add ½ lb of Sugar. Cork & should be ready in 3 months.

# Dandelion Wine

3 lb of Sugar  ❧  3 oranges  ❧  1 gal of Water  ❧  little Yeast  ❧  ½ lb Sugar Candy  ❧  2 or 3 pts of Dandelion Flowers

Put the Sugar in a pan with the juice of Oranges boil the Flowers water & orange Rind for ½ a hour strain over the sugar & work with 2 Tablespoonful of Yeast when lukewarm, this may be put into a Cask in a couple of days & sealed when working over [ie when the yeast has stopped working]. The candy should be crushed. Ready to drink in 3 months & improves by Keeping.

# Elderberry Wine

7 lbs of elderberries  ❧  3 gallons of boiling water  ❧  To each gal of juice allow:-  ❧  3 lbs of Preserving sugar  ❧  1 lb Raisins  ❧  ½ oz of Ground Ginger  ❧  6 cloves  ❧  1 desertspoon of brewer's Yeast or ¼ oz of Compressed yeast  ❧  1 gill of Brandy

Gather the Berries when quite ripe & pick them from stalks. Put into a large Tub bruise them down & pour the boiling Water over. Cover closely & leave for 24 hours. Then strain through a fine Sieve. Measure the Liquid & put into preserving pan. Add Sugar Raisins Ground Ginger & Cloves in the above Proportion bring slowly to the boil & boil for 1 hour skimming when nessesary. Now let the liquid stand until lukewarm then turn into a clean dry cask put in the Yeast spread on a piece of Toast. Cover bung hole with a folded cloth & leave a fortnight then add brandy and bung the Cask tightly. Ready in 6 months.

# Orange Wine

1 gallon water  ❧  3 ½ lb sugar  ❧  12 large Seville Oranges [juice]  ❧  Gill of Brandy  ❧  Tablespoonful of Yeast  ❧  White of egg & shell

Desolve the Sugar in Water with egg & shell crushed & brought to boil, simmer gently for 20 minutes. When nearly cold strain through Jelly bag. Add the strained juice & Yeast & leave the vessel covered for 24 hours. Pour into Cask

bung loosely until fermentation ceases.  Then tighten the bung & allow the Cask to
remain undisturbed for 3 months.  At the end of the time put into another Cask
add Brandy let it remain closely bunged for 12 months, then bottle for use.

# Parsnip Wine

Take 20 lb of parsnips wash & scrub them well.  Put them on to boil in 10 gallons
of cold water boil untill quite soft strain through muslin or a very clean cloth
pressing the parsnips quite dry to every gallon of the parsnip liquor add 3 lbs of
sugar & juice of 2 Lemons & peel.  Boil ½ an hour.  When milk warm spread 2 oz
of German Yeast on Toast cover close, let it stand a week stiring it up every day.
Strain into a Cask.  It will be ready to bottle in 5 or 6 months.

# Plum Wine

To every gallon of Water add 2 ½ lbs Plums 3 lb of Sugar.  Bruise the Plums break
a few stones so that the nut flavour gets into the Wine.  Soak the Plums 24 hours
mash well strain the Liquor, to this Liquor add Sugar, take a little of the Juice &
put into a baisen with a dessertspoonful of Yeast allow this to ferment & add it to
the other Juice.  At the end of 24 hours the whole should be fermented.  Then
place in a Cask & allow to remain until fermentation ceases, about 14 days, then
draw from the Cask & strain though a muslin bag.  Put all back into Cask.  If not
sweet enough add ½ lb of Sugar to the gal, bung tightly, & if there are no further
signs of Fermentation then wine will be ready in 4 months.

# Potato Wine

### To each gallon of water
4 lb Potatoes   ❧   3 ½ lb Demerera Sugar   ❧   1 Lemon   ❧   1 handful of hops
❧   2 oz Yeast

Boil Together potatoes, Lemon & hops, & before they break strain them off & pour
the water in which the Potatoes has been boiled on to the Sugar Demera, when
nearly cold work with Yeast.  By boiling lemon, Potatoes & hops together in a

[muslin] bag much trouble will be avoided if they break.  Next day place wine in a Cask bung tightly & when wine has finished working bung up tightly & it will be ready to bottle in about 3 weeks.

# Raspberry Wine

### *To each gal of water*
4 lb Raspberries   ❧   2 lb Sugar   ❧   ½ teaspoon Cream of Tartar.

Put Raspberries into earthenware Vessell, press well, strain away all juice until Raspberries are dry.  To the juice add sugar & water to make a gallon, take a little of this Juice & put in a basin.  Add one teaspoonful of Yeast & allow to ferment until the Yeast reaches the Top of the baisen, add to rest of Juice.  Put the whole of this into Cask & allow to ferment for 10 days then draw off.  Strain the thick which you will find in the bottom of the Cask, wash out Cask, put whole into it & if wine is not sweet enough, add another ½ lb of Sugar to the Gallon, bung down tightly & in 6 weeks it will be ready to bottle.  Should the wine show a sediment in the bottle, it must be re-bottled.  This wine is now ready for drinking.

# Redcurrant Wine

### *To every gal. of water add*
2 lb Currants   ❧   3 lb Sugar

Remove Currants from Stalks put into earthenware bowl press well & strain off Juice.  To the Juice add the sugar & water to make a gallon, extract a little of the juice & put in a baisen with a dessertspoonful of Yeast.  Allow this to ferment until the yeast gets to the top of the baisen, then add to other Juice.  At the end of 24 hours the whole should be fermented, then put into a Cask & allow to remain until fermentation ceases which will be about 14 days.  Then draw from Cask and strain through Muslin bag, put all back into Cask.  If not sweet enough add ½ lb of Sugar to the gal.  If no sign of further fermentation, ready in 3 months.

# Rhubarb Wine

4 lb Rhubarb ❧ water ❧
Sugar ❧ Yeast ❧ ½ teaspoonful of Cream of Tartar

Cut Rhubarb into dice about an inch leaving on the Skin, put into Preserving Pan, cover it with Water & allow to stand for 30 hours. Strain off water & then squash Rhubarb, until thoroughly dry, put the resultant Liquor with the water already strained off. To every gal of this Liquor add 3 lb of Sugar taking care all is dissolved. Take a little of this Liquor & Juice, put into a basin with a teaspoonful of Yeast allow to ferment until it reaches top of basin. Add to the Juice & Sugar, put into Cask & allow to ferment 21 days. Draw from Cask, strain the thick which you will find at the bottom, was Cask out and put all back. The wine will be ready for use in [one?] month's time, but at the end of the [month], if desirous of keeping it, it will set up a second Fermentation. After that Fermentation ceases the Wine will be much better. If not sweet enough add another ¾ lb of sugar to the Gallon. This wine can be used & flavoured to take the Place of any other wines in this book.

# Sloe Wine

To ❧ 1 gal of Sloes allow ❧ 1 gal Water ❧ 4 lb Preserving Sugar ❧ 1 gill Brandy ❧ ¼ of Isinglass

Gather sloes when quite ripe & use only those that are sound. Pick & wash them carefully put them in Tub pour boiling water over them. Cover & leave for a week stirring daily then add sugar & when disolved put all in clean cask. When Fermentation ceases add brandy. Tie the Isinglass in muslin bag to the bung & bung down tightly. Leave for a year before bottling.

# Sloe Gin

Crush small 3 oz of Sugar Candy place with 3 oz Loaf Sugar place with ½ lb of Sloes to a bottle of Gin in Jar shake daily for 3 months then strain through a Jelly bag. Bottle, keep as long as convenient. Prick sloes before hand.

# Whiskey Wine

3 lb Demera Sugar    ※    1 lb Wheat    ※    1 ½ lb old Potatoes    ※    1 ½ lb
Raisens    ※    1 oz Yeast    ※    1 gal water

Place Sugar, wheat in bag, Potatoes chopped or Grated, raisens in open Tub.  Add
boiling Water & when nearly cold add Yeast, stir every day for 3 weeks, strain pressing all juice out of Raisens.  Place in Cask add a little dissolved Isinglass in about a
month & the wine should be fit to drink shortly after, but improved by keeping.

# Acknowledgements

First, I owe a huge vote of thanks to my team of testers who somehow managed to take time out from very busy lives to help make new recipes out of old. I could never have tested 100+ recipes on my own, so I cannot thank you all enough. You literally made this book possible.

*From the University of Bath Library*
Alison Baud, our resident Scot and Mistress of Marmalade. So what exactly is the problem with *German* shortbread?
Sue Chadwick, who heroically managed to test twelve recipes while her kitchen was literally being rebuilt around her.
Nick Gibbins and Isobel Stark, for whom jams and chutneys hold no terrors.
Sue Gowman, who tackled the recipes nobody else wanted, and found it well worth the effort.
Tina Green, who coined the superb phrase 'sucky toffee'.
Sheila Page, lover of apple puddings and keeper of jelly-moulds.
Kate Robinson, who hosted the Mary Jane Stratton dinner party, and thus deviously recruited three more testers.
Verity Smith, who nobly cooked a fruit cake even though she doesn't like it. And a very fine cake too.
*From Edinburgh*
Helen Williams, biographical research assistant as well as tester of cakes and puddings. *Chto za podruga!*
*From Norwich*
Sarah Hassan, a good friend and inspired cook. But yes, it's a good idea to cook the fish first.
*From Rode*
Helena Cave-Penney and Simon Best, who make the best-decorated, most artistic puddings in the West Country (see front cover).
Alex Sing, who saved the day with her deep-fat fryer, and with it made very fine doughnuts.
*From Sherborne*
Christine Clist, honorary family member and very dear friend.
Rachel-Mary Perry, who probably never imagined that she was coming all the way from New Zealand just to help test recipes.
*From Wantage*
Linda Jordan, my much-loved sister-in-law, quite simply one of the finest cooks ever to come out of Cornwall.

143

*I also would like to those who have helped with other aspects of the book:-*
John Chandler of the Hobnob Press; Mary Jane's niece Rosalind Hiscock; Mrs. Mavis Hutton, who grew up at The Hill, and kindly arranged for us to see it; Chris Phillips (*how* many gravestones?); the graveyard clerk of St Andrew's Church, Clevedon; Geoff Stratton and his phenomenal Stratton genealogical database; Somerset Record Office; Wiltshire & Swindon Record Office; Worcester-shire Record Office; Bath Spa University College Library; and Wiltshire County Local Studies Library. Not forgetting all the family, friends, babies, colleagues, visitors and cricketers who kindly (and, more often than not, enthusiastically) helped taste all the recipes.

Finally, a huge thank you to my mother, Marjorie Jordan, who started it all off by giving me the Receipt-Book, and who has been consultant cook and a fount of family history throughout.

# Bibliography

Beeton, Mrs. (1907).  *Book of household management: a guide to cookery in all its branches.* London: Ward, Lock.

Beeton, Mrs. (1907). *Mrs. Beeton's every-day cookery.* New ed. London: Ward, Lock.

Brunning, Jane (2000). *Beckhampton: a village through time.* Privately published.

*Dictionary of national biography.*

Horn, Pamela (1989). *The Victorian and Edwardian schoolchild.* Gloucester: Alan Sutton.

Horn, Pamela (2001). *Life below stairs in the 20th century.* Stroud: Sutton.

Huggett, Frank E. (1977). *Life below stairs: domestic servants in England from Victorian times.* London: John Murray.

*Kelly's Directory of Wiltshire* (1903). London: Kelly's Directories.

Pasley, Rodney (1982). *'Send Malcolm': the life of Major-General Sir John Malcolm 1769-1833.* London: BACSA.

Post Office, *Appointments of rural postmen.* Wiltshire & Swindon Record Office (WSRO) 3144/2/2

Sim, Andrew (1993). *English racing stables.* Addlestone: Dial.

*Who was who 1897-1915* (1988).

*Woodborough CE School log book 1873-1917.* WSRO F8/500/297/1/1.

# Index

*This is an index of recipes and principal ingredients, and of people and places. Commonplace and minor ingredients are not indexed.*

## A

Alton Barnes (Wilts)  xi, xiii, xv, 13, 97
Alton Priors (Wilts)  xvii
Alverstoke (Hants)  97
Amelia, Princess  27
anchovy
  essence  9
  paste  5, 7, 16
angelica  51
apple, apples
  beer  136
  chutney  105
  cooking  27, 28, 41, 112, 122
  eating  115
  jelly  63, 125
  prepared  43
  wine  136
apricot
  eggs  66
  jam  28, 45, 121
Ashfield pudding  38

## B

Bachelor's pudding  43
bacon  6
baked puddings  19-32
Beacon Hill (Wilts)  xiii
beans, French  118
Beckhampton (Wilts) xiii, 130

beers  135-6
Beeton, Mrs *passim*
beetroot
  chutney  112
  wine  136
biscuits, boudoir  51
blackberry
  jam  122
  pudding  40
  wine  136
blackcurrant wine  137
boiled
  puddings  33-47
  sweets  133
boudoir biscuits  51
Bournemouth  111
brandy  46, 115
bread
  crumbs  7, 43, 44, 45
  stale  8, 22
Bristol University  xviii
Burton (Cheshire)  13
butter, coffee  75

## C

cabinet pudding  51
cakes  67-102
canapées, cheese  17
capers  16
caramel pudding  54

carrot wine  137
cheese
  cake, lemon  131
  canapées  17
  Cheddar  3, 12
  soufflé  12
cherries  85
  glacé  51, 80, 99
chicken  3, 5
chillies  105, 107
chocolate
  cakes  88
  cream  56
  icing  89
  pudding  35
Christmas pudding  46
chutneys  103-18
Clevedon (Som) xiii, 116
cocoa  36
coconut, dessicated  80
coffee
  butter 75
  icing  75
Coggins family x, xv-xx
 -John Edwin (Ned) xv-xx
  Marjorie  xvi-xx
  Mary Jane *passim*
  Stanley  xv-xx
cream  3, 7, 14
  chocolate  56
Crystal Palace pudding  53
currants  43, 46, 83, 91, 99, 100, 101,
    115
custard  22, 23, 54
  set  51, 53

D
damson, damsons
  bottled  117
  wine  137
dandelion wine  138

Darling family  130
  Fred  130
  Sam  130
  Violetta  130
Derbyshire pudding  25
desserts, set  49-66
devilling  5
Devizes (Wilts)  26
Devonshire pudding  28
doughnuts  95
drop cakes  91
Dundee marmalade  128

E
Eastman, Sarah (Mrs Sladen)  13
egg, eggs
  apricot  66
  hard boiled  14
  jelly  64
elderberry wine  138
Ellis, Clough Williams xvii
Eva's beetroot chutney  112

F
Fearon, Mrs  9
Felce
  Gilbert  111
  Mrs  (Hilda Stratton)110, 111, 118
fig pudding  44
fish  7, 9
  pulled  7
  soufflé  9
fruit cake  102
Fry, Sir Geoffrey  xvii

G
Gale, Mrs  57, 90
Genoese pastry  85
German
  pound cake  100
  shortbread  92

Giddings, Charlotte (Lottie Lee) 97
ginger 39
  bread cake viii, 82
  ground 105, 109
  jam 39
  rhubarb 123
gooseberry, gooseberries 31
  bottled 117
  jelly 126
  turnovers 31, 58
green tomato
  chutney 110
  jam 132

H

ham 17
Hawkins family 113-14
  Eva (Stratton) 113-14
Hiscock, Rosalind xix
Honeystreet (Wilts) xi, xvi, 13, 113, 114
hot tomato chutney 107
Hughes family 116

I

icing
  chocolate 89
  coffee 75
Indian toast 16
Iris pudding 36

J

jam, jams 38, 85, 119-32
  apricot 28, 45
  rhubarb and ginger 39
  sandwich 69
jellies 49-66, 119-32
Johnson
  Sir Charles 47
  Lady Jemima 47-8
Jordan family x, xix

K

Kealey, Dr Jonathan 97

L

lavender 51
Leicester xix
lemon, lemons 23, 25, 41, 44, 57, 63,
    64, 77, 84, 87, 100
  cake 84
  cheese cake 131
  cream 60
  Jif 43
  solid 62
Lottie's doughnuts 95
Loveredge, Mrs 46

M

macaroni 3
Madeira cake 23, 77
main courses 1-17
Malcolm family 116-17
  Sir George 116
  Lady Wilhelmina 47-8, 115, 116-17
Manchester cake 80
Manningford Bohune (Wilts) xi, 111,
    113
Marlborough (Wilts) xviii
marmalade 21, 119-32
  Dundee 128
  pudding (baked) 22
  pudding (steamed) 37
marrow 118
  vegetable, pickled 118
Marshall family x, xi, 113
Martin family 47
meringue 23
Meyrick, Mrs 92
military tartlets 85
mincemeat 115
mocha cake 73
Mortimer (Berks) xv

mustard 5, 7, 14, 17, 107

**N**
Nash, Paul 111
Nassaw pudding 21
Norwich cake 101

**O**
Oare (Wilts) xv, xvi, 120
onions 107, 110, 112
orange, oranges 128
  cake 78
  pudding 23
  solid 62
  wine 138

**P**
Paradise pudding 41
Parker, Mrs 101
parsnip wine 139
pastry
  Genoese 85
  puff 3, 31
  short crust 25
peel, candied 99, 100, 101
Phyllis's
  lemon cake 84
  queen cakes 87
  sponge cake 70
pistachio nuts 66
plum wine 139
port 6, 115
  mock 136
potato wine 139
pound cake 99, 100
preserves 103-18
Princess Amelia's puddings 27
puddings
  baked 19-32
  boiled 33-47
  steamed 33-47

pulled fish 7

**Q**
queen cakes 87

**R**
rabbit 6
raisins 41, 46, 105, 109, 115
raspberry
  sponge 59
  wine 140
Reading (Berks) xix
redcurrant wine 140
rhubarb 31, 39
  bottled 117
  ginger 123
  jam 39
  sponge 57
  turnovers 31, 58
  wine 141
rice cakes 90
Roman pie 3
Rose's
  pound cake 99
  sultana cake 98

**S**
salad dressing 14
sandwich, jam 69
savouries 1-17
Scarborough cake 83
schools xi-xiii, xviii, 26
scones 94
set desserts 49-66
Severn cup pudding 45
sherry 53
shortbread, German 92
Sladen
  Rev Charles 13
  Evelyn 13
  Mrs (Sarah Eastman) 12, 13, 14

sloe
  gin 141
  wine 141
Smith
  Miss S L xii
  Mrs 118
soufflé
  cheese 12
  fish 9
  tomato 10
Southsea (Hants) 13
spirits 135, 141-2
sponge
  cakes 70
  fingers 35, 51, 53, 57
  rhubarb 57
Stanton St Bernard (Wilts) xix
steamed puddings 33-47
stewed rabbit 6
Stratton family x, xi-xix, 111, 114
  Eva 113-14
  Frederick xi
  Hannah xi
  Harold 113-14
  Hilda (Mrs Felce) 111
  Mary Jane, her life xi-xx
  Rose 97
suet 37
  vegetable 44
sultana, sultanas 45, 84, 87, 99, 100
  cake 98
  pudding 29
sweet tomato chutney 109
sweets, boiled 133
Swiss roll 71
syrup, golden 40

T
tartlets, military 85
toast, Indian 16
toffee 134
tomato, tomatoes 10
  chutney 107, 109, 110
  jam 132
  soufflé 10
treacle, black 82
trifle sponges 53
turnovers, gooseberry and rhubarb 31,
  58

U
Upton on Severn (Worcs) xiii, 47-8

V
vanilla pod 51

W
Warburton, Arthur 97
whiskey wine 142
Whitecliffe (Dorset) 111
Whitting
  Ernest xii, 26
  Horatio 26
Winchester (Hants) 111
wine, wines 46
  country 135-42
Woodborough (Wilts) xi-xiii, xv, xix,
  26, 97
Woolfrey, Mrs 117